Emotional
Intelligence
for ROOKIES

Titles in the *for* ROOKIES series

About the authors

Andrea Bacon is co-founder and research director of Inspiring Perform-ance. Specializing in leadership, emotional intelligence and sustaining com-petitive advantage, Andrea regularly inspires business audiences by drawing on the powerful, stimulating and pragmatic lessons she has learned. She also coaches and develops senior business executives and has co-authored two leadership books. Andrea started her career in media and communica-tions, and then competed in the 1996/7 BT Global Challenge Round the World Yacht Race. She subsequently set up a research forum with Henley Management College and used the 2000/1 BT Global Challenge as a live case study, focusing on emotional intelligence and its impact on leadership, performance and culture. Andrea can be contacted at andreabacon@ inspiringperformance.com or through www.inspiringperformance.com.

Ali Dawson, MD of Total Dynamix, specializes in improving personal performance through emotional intelligence, both in sport and business. Her focus within business is in coaching individuals to add greater value through more effective leadership behaviour and skills, and by building more productive working relationships with others. Ali's clients are many and varied; personal and professional; public and private sector; local and global. Projects she has been involved with include working with BT Global Challenge Yacht Race, The England Rugby Team and The Royal Military Academy, Sandhurst. Ali is a senior consultant with both Inspir-ing Performance Ltd and The Worklife Company Ltd. To contact Ali, email info@totaldynamix.eclipse.co.uk

Emotional Intelligence

for ROOKIES

First published in 2010 by Marshall Cavendish Business
An imprint of Marshall Cavendish International
PO Box 65829
London EC1P 1NY
United Kingdom
info@marshallcavendish.co.uk
and
1 New Industrial Road
Singapore 536196
genrefsales@sg.marshallcavendish.com
www.marshallcavendish.com/genref

A member of **BPR**

businesspublishersroundtable.com

Marshall Cavendish is a trademark of Times Publishing Limited

Other Marshall Cavendish offices: Marshall Cavendish International (Asia) Private Limited, 1 New Industrial Road, Singapore 536196 • Marshall Cavendish Corporation. 99 White Plains Road, Tarrytown NY 10591–9001, USA • Marshall Cavendish International (Thailand) Co Ltd. 253 Asoke, 12th Floor, Sukhumvit 21 Road, Klongtoey Nua, Wattana, Bangkok 10110, Thailand • Marshall Cavendish (Malaysia) Sdn Bhd, Times Subang, Lot 46, Subang Hi-Tech Industrial Park, Batu Tiga, 40000 Shah Alam, Selangor Darul Ehsan, Malaysia

A CIP record for this book is available from the British Library

ISBN 978-0-462-09979-8

Illustrations by Nuria Aparicio and Joan Guardiet

Printed and bound in Singapore by Fabulous Printers Pte Ltd

Contents

Introduction

Have you ever walked away from a situation or finished a conversation which has left you feeling frustrated, embarrassed, angry or upset, asking yourself:

- "What was that all about?"
- "Why did they react in that way?"
- "Why on earth did I say that?"
- "Why am I feeling like this?"

You may not know the reason why this interaction didn't go well, but your feelings will have been triggered by the discord, affecting your physiology and emotional state. With your internal state in disarray, you may have found it difficult to think clearly for some time afterwards, and you may even have said or done something that you later regretted.

Emotions are powerful things! If they are not managed intelligently they can sweep you off course, affecting your health, happiness and success.

Emotional Intelligence for Rookies is about developing your emotional intelligence (or EI for short). It helps you to understand where

2 your emotions come from, how they affect you, and more importantly how you can use them to your advantage.

In today's turbulent business environment, using your emotional intelligence alongside your rational intelligence gives you a competitive edge. By embracing your emotional intelligence you will be more aware of yourself, more in tune with others and better able to create a sustainable personal culture.

This book specifically looks at how you can develop yourself and your relationships with others by:

- Understanding your emotional state and physiology.
- Overcoming life's ups and downs.
- Increasing energy levels; both yours and others'.
- Enhancing your relationships.
- Tailoring your words and actions to resonate with others.
- Trusting and valuing your intuition.
- Performing consistently.

How to read this book

This is a practical textbook for developing emotional intelligence, incorporating useful tips and powerful development activities. It is designed to take you on a journey of self-discovery, bringing your emotional intelligence to life and creating your personal culture.

To maximize this experience you need to have an openness, willingness and curiosity, unhindered by any preconceived ideas that you may have about emotional intelligence.

We suggest that you use a dedicated notebook and adopt the following approach in order to gain maximum benefit from the content:

1. Chapters 1 and 2 should be read first in order to help you understand how your mind and body interact. With this knowledge you will be better placed to work with

the specific EI elements and appreciate what you are trying to address.

2. By completing the EI Questionnaire in Chapter 2, you will have a better understanding of your own level of emotional intelligence. This will provide you with a starting point for your personal development.

3. At the end of Chapter 2 you will find the EI Energy Generator, on which you can plot your current level of emotional intelligence. As you move through the book and enhance your understanding, you will be encouraged to re-evaluate your initial perception.

4. Chapters 3 to 9 provide the practical tools for developing your EI. Each chapter is built around one of the seven elements of the Higgs & Dulewicz EI framework (see Appendix), and explores its relevance and importance in today's dynamic environment.

   Taking each element in turn, you'll be able to identify your own strengths or needs, and assess the impact you have on others, both positively and negatively.

5. Next read Chapter 3 and focus on your self-awareness to develop a greater sense of how you handle your emotions. Increase this understanding in discussion with others who could help you to identify the priority elements for your development.

6. Having identified your priorities, explore Chapters 4–9. You will notice that all of the elements are interrelated and consequently, wherever you stop and focus your attention, you are likely to experience a positive "knock on" effect in your overall EI.

   In Chapters 4–9 you will find a number of exercises. Invest time in completing these. The exercises are designed to stimulate your feelings and thoughts and give you an opportunity to reflect on what you do. They may appear simplistic, but try them out – you'll be surprised at how much you learn about yourself and how you affect others.

7. Chapter 10 demonstrates the personal culture that you can create when you fully embrace all of the elements of emotional intelligence. By this time you will be in tune with how you feel and more aware of your impact on others, and you will have a natural ability to energize yourself and others around you.

4   8. At the back of the book, you will find the Appendix, with the
     Higgs & Dulewicz Seven Elements of EI, further useful tools and
     suggested reading material.

Making the most of your time

Make it personal
To really gain an understanding of what you are reading, you need to
draw on your personal experience. Reflect on previous "real life" scenarios and consider what you could have done differently.

Seek input from others
Consider feedback as a gift! Someone else's perception provides you
with an insightful, more rounded and useful view. Be willing to listen
and take their view on board. It may help you to identify specific areas
for your development.

Gain support
This is crucial to your success both as you go through this book and in
the future. Recruit your friends, family, partner and work colleagues if
you believe that they will provide you with sound input.

Be realistic 5

As with anything, the value of the learning is in the application.

To ensure your success, consider carefully which areas to select for your development. Identify the quick wins; in other words, those small changes or tweaks that you can make immediately, and which will begin to make a difference. Consider the bigger challenges and prioritize your goals. Don't be over-ambitious; one thing at a time. Whatever you decide, keep it simple, and remember: practice is the key.

Keep going

Changing habits and behaviour doesn't happen overnight, so identify techniques you can apply daily in a range of situations. Keep practising for 28 days. Once your new habit has moved from your conscious into your subconscious mind, you'll be surprised at how natural it will feel.

Ask others if they have noticed any change!

Consider someone who positively affects your life; who inspires you, who you respect, who you connect with and whose company you enjoy. Perhaps your best ever boss, colleague or client. This may be a relationship from the past, or one that exists today. Why does this person come to the forefront of your mind? What is it about this person that sets them apart from others; what do they specifically do; how do they interact? Make a note of your thoughts in your notebook now.

CHAPTER 1

Bringing emotional intelligence to life – through your mind

What is emotional intelligence?

What makes someone stand out? As the thoughts that you have written down will show, it's not just one thing, but a combination of personal attributes. In fact, it's *emotional intelligence*.

Many people think emotional intelligence is soft and fluffy, and if it had a colour they would probably say it was pink! Right now, you might feel the same, but since you are reading *Emotional Intelligence for Rookies*, you are probably ready to explore the concept and look at how to practically apply your own emotional intelligence.

The fact is, everyone is emotionally intelligent to some degree, but whether you choose to act with emotional intelligence depends on whether you believe in and value your feelings; and on whether you understand the impact emotional intelligence has in your life today.

This chapter highlights the essence of emotional intelligence and draws together the many strands associated with its definition. It explores "intrapersonal" and "interpersonal" intelligences and gives a basic explanation of how the emotional brain works in harmony with the cognitive brain.

Through illustrating some of the challenges of today's dynamic environment, you will realize that emotional intelligence is neither soft nor fluffy and most definitely is not pink. You will recognize that acting with emotional intelligence is the way to enhance your personal performance and to succeed when working with others.

Rookie Buster

Acting with emotional intelligence is the way to enhance your personal performance and to succeed when working with others.

To help explain and remove some of the myths associated with EI, there is a need to accept that emotional intelligence is not one thing. It is about understanding emotions, impulses and drivers, and intelligently handling these to enhance performance and relationships.

Your ability to act with emotional intelligence depends on your level of emotional maturity. Maturity comes from wisdom gained through experience, combined with an increased understanding of yourself and an insight into how you may interact with others.

This knowledge, gained on your personal journey through life, explains why your emotional intelligence increases with age and experience.

Rookie Buster

Your emotional intelligence increases with age and experience.

In 1990, Peter Salovey and Jack Meyer were the first to adopt the term "emotional intelligence" to describe the way people bring "intelligence" to their emotions. Since then, many others, such as Dr Daniel Goleman (in the USA) and Professors Malcolm Higgs and Victor Dulewicz (in the UK) have offered a definition for emotional intelligence. These are best summarized as follows.

Emotional intelligence is about being able to:

- Recognize your own feelings and those of others.
- Lift your mood and motivate yourself.
- Manage your emotions internally and in your relationships with others.

Self and relationship management

From the summary definition, you can see that the first aspect of emotional intelligence is related to your ability to manage yourself. To do this you need to have a strong sense of self-awareness, a belief in yourself and firm self-control.

The second aspect of emotional intelligence is related to your ability to manage your relationships with others. For this you need to really understand the feelings and responses of others and build on this understanding to form strong and lasting relationships.

To help you to develop self and relationship management, you'll need to tap into your "intrapersonal" and "interpersonal" intelligences.

These are just two of your multiple intelligences, researched by Howard Gardner, Harvard Professor of Education Emeritus, and discussed in his book *Frames of Mind*.

Intrapersonal intelligence

Through using your intrapersonal intelligence (or self-knowledge), you can identify what is going on inside you, and consider what you need to do. Intrapersonal intelligence helps to make sense of the things you do, the thoughts you have and the feelings you feel. With intrapersonal intelligence you can begin to take control of yourself and your emotions.

> **Rookie Buster**
>
> With intrapersonal intelligence you can begin to take control of yourself and your emotions.

Interpersonal intelligence

Through your interpersonal intelligence (or knowledge of dealing with other people), you can be intelligent in identifying what other people are feeling and also the feelings between others. You can therefore make intelligent decisions about what you need to do about that. It can help you to stay in tune with others, empathize, communicate and influence. With interpersonal intelligence you can inspire others and develop trust.

> **Rookie Buster**
>
> With interpersonal intelligence you can inspire others and develop trust.

Cognitive versus emotional intelligence

Historically, human intelligence has been based on cognitive intelligence, and from the early twentieth century onwards intelligence quotient, or IQ, tests have been available to measure cognitive ability and intellect. With school systems around the world geared towards valuing and developing the logical-mathematical and linguistic capabilities, IQ alone was widely believed to be the best predictor of success.

However, over more recent years, research by a number of psychologists has led to the belief that there are a number of qualities other than IQ that determine success. These capabilities largely relate to the ability to get on with other people, and can be defined as emotional intelligence.

In 1996, Dr Daniel Goleman brought the concept of emotional intelligence to the attention of the world when he published his first book *Emotional Intelligence – Why It Can Matter More Than IQ*. His book became a bestseller as people showed their willingness to accept that IQ on its own was not a reliable predictor of success in most areas of life.

Goleman partly supported his case for EI being "an important predictor of managerial performance" by studying the physiological basis of EI. However, his strongest belief in the supremacy of EI over IQ and technical capability came from a study in 1998 that analysed competency models from 188 global businesses.

Since that time, other psychologists have collected evidence to support a relationship between emotional intelligence, career progression and performance. It is now widely accepted that EI is twice as important as IQ and technical skills in determining job success.

Rookie Buster

EI is twice as important as IQ and technical skills in determining job success.

12 *Understanding how the brain functions*

Today, through the work of many neurologists and psychologists, much more is understood about the workings of the brain and its interconnections with the bodily systems. While there is still much more that is likely to be revealed in years to come, this book sets out the knowledge that is widely accepted today.

The brain is divided into three distinct areas: frontal, mid and stem. The frontal and mid sections are connected by neural pathways, which allow the cognitive and emotional brains to work together to identify and manage responses to situations. The brain stem is responsible for basic bodily functions, which we do not need to consider here.

Frontal brain

The neo-cortex sits at the top of the brain, above the cortex. "Neo", meaning new, defines this area of the cognitive brain that is unique to humans and has evolved over many centuries, since man first needed to plan, organize and interact with others.

Today the neo-cortex is a very sophisticated machine that governs analytical and technical ability. It is a highly efficient learning area that grasps concepts quickly and expands understanding by linking new ideas or facts.

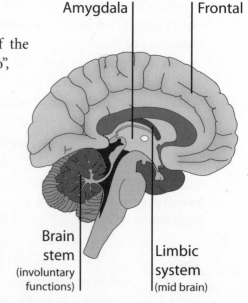

Amygdala | Frontal

Brain stem (involuntary functions) | Limbic system (mid brain)

Mid brain

This is the site of the emotional brain: the amygdala and the limbic system that governs feelings, impulses and drives.

Skills learned here are embedded through motivation, extended practice and feedback. Many of the techniques within this book are focused on this emotional centre. Learning in this area of the brain is generally slower than in the cognitive brain, as it involves re-educating the emotional brain and sometimes involves changing deeply ingrained habits. However, because this learning is practised and repeated over time, it is much more likely to be retained and remembered for many years.

Rookie Buster

Because this learning is practised and repeated over time, it is much more likely to be retained and remembered for many years.

Cognitive and emotional brain working in harmony

The fact that the cognitive brain is used to make sense of things often leads to the misconception that it is more powerful than the emotional brain. However, research has shown that it is our emotional brain and limbic system that is the real powerhouse.

While learning may be slower in the emotional brain, the limbic system is constantly gathering information and has the ability to process vast quantities of data – 6 billion bits per second, compared with the cognitive mind that processes just 10–100 bits per second.

14

Rookie Buster

The limbic system is constantly gathering information and has the ability to process vast quantities of data – 6 billion bits per second.

This capacity for collecting and assessing large amounts of information is highly significant. It allows the emotional brain to constantly communicate with all the bodily systems, sensing what is going on and continuously checking new information against stored data, and updating accordingly.

Let's take a simple example to illustrate the importance of this powerhouse. Imagine that you are having a conversation with an important client. Your cognitive centre is working hard, listening to the concept that the client is sharing with you, interpreting the facts, questioning, probing and creating ideas to enable you to respond.

While this is happening your emotional brain is equally busy, collecting and interpreting information from your key sensory systems (eyes, ears, touch, mouth, nose), as well as communicating with your internal systems (heart, gut, lungs, nerves, endocrine and immune).

Your emotional brain is reading your client's face, listening to the tone and rhythm of their voice and tuning in to how they are feeling as you converse. The messages your emotional brain is receiving may range from "He liked that," to "Now he's bored," or "He doesn't agree."

Your emotional brain is also interpreting your bodily transmissions – the pressure wave from your gut is getting stronger, your heart rate is increasing, your blood is rushing to your face.   15

Interpreting all this at high speed, your emotional brain is able to feed your cognitive brain, allowing you to make changes to your style and to fine tune what you say next.

Using your intrapersonal and interpersonal intelligences to take control

Now you have an understanding of the basic functioning of your brain and the role that the emotional centre has in providing crucial data and information to the thinking brain. You can now begin to see the importance of how you must manage your intrapersonal and interpersonal intelligence.

Most of the time you will not be conscious of the intelligence gathered by your senses from external sources, or gathered by the limbic system from your internal sources. However, this is happening second by second and could, if recognized, provide you with a wealth of data on which to base your decisions, your judgements and your responses.

By bringing a conscious awareness to this emotional data, you can start to use this information more practically and take control of how you feel, think and act.

Why is emotional intelligence important?

Emotional intelligence is primarily about managing yourself well and enhancing your relationships with others in order to be happier, healthier and more successful. This concept is not new, and neither is the concept of emotional intelligence. It's a fact that human beings strive to achieve happiness, stay healthy and attain personal success, relative to their environment.

16

Rookie Buster

Emotional intelligence is primarily about managing yourself well and enhancing your relationships with others in order to be happier, healthier and more successful.

So what has brought emotional intelligence to the forefront in recent years, and why is it important to recognize and use the power of emotional intelligence today?

Let's take a look at some of the challenges that drive the need for greater emotional intelligence today. Consider these in terms of self and relationship management.

Self-management

A changing world

Uncertainty and turbulence is nothing new. For nearly thirty years industrialized countries have seen the pace of change increasing and the pressures mounting, as technology and communications have developed and enhanced.

Individuals have faced continual uncertainty as organizations change size and shape, expand into new geographical markets and introduce new methodologies and technologies to replace tried and tested practices.

This period of evolution has been and is extremely dynamic, and the future will be the same.

Economic drivers have also changed, moving from transactional (what you do), to knowledge based (what you know). Today the economy is driven by relationships and how you relate to others.

Rookie Buster

Today the economy is driven by relationships and how you relate to others.

Consequently, individuals require higher levels of self-awareness, self-belief, self-control and self-motivation to cope with and accept continual change, respond flexibly and manage their anxieties and stress. They also need to develop a deep understanding of how to effectively relate and successfully interact with others.

Sophisticated technology

With significant advances in technology, there is less need to work from a dedicated office, or use wires to connect to information systems; access to data and knowledge is available from wherever you work, whether it be at a home office, a train station or a hotel foyer; 24/7, worldwide!

But advances bring new challenges: the speed of communication, the availability and volume of information, heightened expectations in terms of response times or decision making, and increased pressure to stay ahead of the competition.

Such challenges increase the need for individuals to manage themselves effectively, heightening the need for self-awareness, intuitiveness and conscientiousness.

Organizational structure

As organizational structures have flattened, individuals have seen their remits broaden and their levels of responsibility increase. With no hierarchical structure, individuals are often working without direction, reporting to line managers who have no relevant knowledge and

18   who could be physically located elsewhere or working in a different time zone.

Individuals may feel daunted, isolated and overloaded by this new business environment. With limited personal training and lack of leadership training they may find it difficult to cope with the pressures, becoming overwhelmed and often ill.

If you are working in this type of environment, you need to be acutely self-aware and to develop high levels of emotional resilience.

Rookie Buster

You need to be acutely self-aware and to develop high levels of emotional resilience.

Relationship management

Understanding and retaining clients

Clients and customers are faced with an extraordinary plethora of choice and have unlimited access to information. Consequently their expectations have heightened, their requirements have become more sophisticated, and they are clearly more savvy when it comes to negotiating the best deal.

These factors mean that it is more important than ever to develop client relationships through openness, honesty and trust. They emphasize the need to create mutual respect and embrace a collaborative approach.

In theory this sounds simple, but in practice it can only be achieved with genuine interpersonal skills, by being attuned to the non-verbalized needs of the clients and being sensitive to one's own words and actions.

Rookie Buster

It is more important than ever to develop client relationships through openness, honesty and trust.

Working cross-culturally

Operating in a global environment, working cross-culturally and multi-functionally, creates a far greater dynamic and challenge for individuals and organizations today. Cultural style differences often don't transcend borders, and difficulties arise when this is not understood.

Being emotionally intelligent creates an awareness and understanding that attunes individuals to the feelings, needs and styles of others. Even if there is no common language, much can be picked up through facial expressions, body language and inferences. Being able to tune in to these subtle changes is critical to creating rapport, getting people on side and working together successfully.

Rookie Buster

Being emotionally intelligent creates an awareness and understanding that attunes individuals to the feelings, needs and styles of others.

Coach's notes

This chapter has explained the essence of emotional intelligence and how the brain captures and interprets this intelligence. It has highlighted why EI is so important in today's dynamic environment, and sets out a framework for assessing and developing EI.

Before you take any steps to practically enhance your own emotional intelligence, it is worth remembering:

- Emotional intelligence is twice as important as IQ, and as you become more senior within an organization, your emotional intelligence becomes more important.
- Your emotional brain can and will override your cognitive brain if you are not "in tune" and "in control" of your emotions.
- To enhance your personal performance you need to recognize and control your emotions, drivers and impulses.
- To work with others and enhance results, you need to be attuned to their feelings and interpret the signals that you receive.

Go for it! Having got this far, you should now feel pleased that you have made sense of emotional intelligence in a rational, logical way by using your cognitive intelligence. Now it is time for you to turn to Chapter 2, tune in to your body and begin to have that mind/body conversation, so that you can feel, think and act in a more emotionally intelligent way.

Tuning in to your body may sound strange and may even make you feel uncomfortable at this point. Perhaps you have never really given much thought to the fact that on some days you feel positive and enthusiastic, and on other days quite apathetic and low.

As you move through this chapter, you will explore what is happening within your body and what is behind your feelings or your state of mind. You will start to understand what creates an emotion, the different types of feelings and the distinction between a feeling and a mood.

By the end of this chapter you will know what triggers emotion and how that emotion can affect you. You will realize that there is a constant dialogue going on internally between your body and your mind and recognize that you can be part of that dialogue if you "tune in". By "tuning in" and trusting your feelings, you can really capitalize on what they are telling you and act in a more emotionally intelligent way.

CHAPTER 2

Bringing emotional intelligence to life – through your body

The human body

The human body is an incredibly complex and integrated web of systems that is still not completely understood today. However, advances in technology and multiple fields of scientific research over the last two decades have helped scientists understand more about how these systems impact on one another, how they communicate with one another and the brain, and how they affect our emotional state, our health and our personal performance.

To try to understand these complicated connections, let's start with some biology. Being "alive" means that our bodily systems are continually functioning, each creating a unique stream of information that is communicated between the body and the brain.

This information is transmitted in a variety of ways, determined by your physiology or your biochemistry. For example, your organs, such as heart, lungs, liver, gut and kidneys, transmit electrical, electromagnetic and chemical signals, while your systems, such as immune, nervous and endocrine, transmit pressure, sound or heat waves.

Rookie Buster

Being "alive" means that our bodily systems are continually functioning, each creating a unique stream of information that is communicated between the body and the brain.

With all these streams of information passing around your body, it is not surprising that your body is in a constant state of flux as energy is created and moves through it.

What is emotion?

Emotion is sometimes explained as energy in motion (that is, "e-motion"), referring to the shifting energy within the body. This shift in energy is a signal to the brain. Once the brain has received this cue, it is able to interpret the emotion into a feeling and start to prepare the body for action.

For example – you are walking along and look up to see an overhead sign swinging wildly on its fixings. Internally, certain neurons and hormones are triggered; the brain recognizes the energy (e-motion) created by these and brings this to your consciousness. Consequently you feel fear and you jump out of the way.

Most emotions will be fleeting, and will therefore remain below the level of consciousness. However, when emotions come into the consciousness they are experienced as feelings.

Where do emotions come from?

There has been, and continues to be, considerable debate about where emotions come from. Do emotions start in the body and influence the brain? Does the brain conceive emotion and influence the body? Or is it possible that they can start in either the body or the brain?

Jack Meyer said: "An emotion occurs when there are certain bio-   25
logical, certain experiential and certain cognitive states which all occur
simultaneously."

And according to the neuroscientist Antonia Damasio, emotion is
"an awareness of the current state of the body". Therefore Damasio
would say that emotions come from within and are the brain's interpretation of the internal state.

Rookie Buster

Emotions come from within and are the brain's
interpretation of the internal state.

That's not to say that the external environment has no part to play
in terms of evoking emotion. Sensory information, such as what is
being seen or heard, or the perception of what is happening around,
can create a change within the body. For example, if you were to see a
colleague walking towards you in an aggressive manner, this image
would provoke a reaction within your nervous system and would
affect your internal state. The brain would then receive patterns of data
from the nerve cells and interpret the emotion of fear.

Thoughts and memories can also trigger emotions. Thinking about
a frightening event can activate the same neural and hormonal reactions as actually seeing something that evokes fear. For example, by
thinking about someone behaving aggressively, you can physically
experience the emotion of fear. You may even have experienced this
through reading a good thriller.

Similarly, recalling a specific memory can recreate powerful emotions too. Reflect for a minute on a particularly happy event or joyous
moment in your life; for example, your graduation ceremony, the day
you got the job you really wanted, or your wedding day. Create the
scene in your mind and, if you can, rekindle the emotion; perhaps joy,
happiness or pride.

26 *What role do emotions play?*

Emotions give situations meaning. Without emotions, you would react spontaneously and robotically to events around you, with no control over your response. You would not be able to influence outcomes or achieve your goals or desires.

Having emotions means new information that is received is assessed and evaluated in relation to your past experiences, your ambitions and your desire. The emotion prepares your body and you are then able to act in a manner that is beneficial to you and to the situation.

Emotions are crucial to learning and memory. They motivate you toward seeking new knowledge and achieving rewards. They also help you to avoid harm and distress.

Rookie Buster

Emotions are crucial to learning and memory. They motivate you toward seeking new knowledge and achieving rewards.

Emotions are also key to your social communication. Your facial expression, tone of voice and even your body language will convey to others something of what you are thinking and feeling. Around the world, across cultures, there is remarkable consistency in our facial expressions associated with certain feelings like happiness, fear and anger.

What is a feeling?

Feelings stem from your energy in motion (e-motion) and become real through your mind's subjective awareness. The degree of awareness of your feelings varies depending on how in tune you are with your body. Some people are more aware of what they are feeling than others are. You may remember a colleague saying something like, "Are you feeling OK today? You don't seem yourself." Sometimes, it is not until another person has commented that you stop and reflect on how you are feeling.

Let's look at three different types of feeling.

1. Physiological feeling

You will be familiar with the feeling of being cold, hungry or tired. The relevant bodily area or system will have communicated this to your brain through temperature waves, pressure waves or glucose levels. It is also likely that you will have experienced hot, sweaty palms, a knot in your stomach or shortness of breath when you have been in a state of anxiety or felt under pressure. At one time or another you will certainly have felt your heart beating faster, perhaps when you have unexpectedly been asked to join a meeting to give your opinion.

These physiological feelings can be very strong, and your heartbeat is one of the most powerful signals that your brain receives. Later in this chapter you will see just how it can affect you. In Chapter 4 you will then learn how you can control your heart rate effectively through your breathing.

2. Intuitive feeling

You may well experience those moments of "knowingness". Perhaps you use the term "gut feeling", or intuition. It's on those occasions that you may feel you have a sixth sense. This is an intuitive feeling that comes from within. It's a stored emotional memory, linked to a previous experience. Intuitive feelings can be very powerful. Being in tune and learning to trust these feelings can not only assist in decision making, but is also especially important when dealing with people.

3. Emotional feeling

You'll regularly experience the six basic emotions of:
- Happiness.
- Disgust.
- Surprise.
- Sadness.
- Anger.
- Fear.

You may well be able to label a plethora of others.

The English language has between 3,000 and 4,000 labels for different emotional states, both positive and negative, and these verbal labels try to convey what the emotion is like as an experience.

Each of your emotional feelings will be characterized very differently and will move through different parts of your body. Being able to define a specific feeling and recognize its energy path is important, and means that you can:
- Recreate positive emotions and become more resourceful.
- Distinguish subtle differences between emotions like frustration and annoyance; and therefore choose the most appropriate response/action.

Have a look at the exercise on the next page and begin to characterize your emotions.

Exercise – Describing your feelings

Identify a positive feeling that you are familiar with. Let's take pride as an example.

1. Recall a time you felt very proud.
2. Relive the moment and feel your pride (you may find it easier to close your eyes).
3. Now ask yourself:
   - Where is it located?
   - What size is it?
   - What colour is it?
   - Is there any sound?
   - Is there any associated temperature?
   - How intense is this feeling?
   - How is it moving through my body?
   - How does it move away from my body?
   - Is there any special feature?
4. Jot your description down in a notebook and add other familiar positive feelings, such as enthusiasm or curiosity.
5. Once you are familiar with a feeling, practise turning it on. After a while, it will become so easy you'll be able to do it whenever you need to!

How can emotions affect you and others?

Your mood

A mood is a state of mind that tends to be relatively long lasting. Moods differ from emotions in that they are less specific, are less intense and less likely to be triggered by a particular stimulus or event. The cause of a mood can be hours, days or even weeks old. You can't stop a mood from coming on, but you can control it and how long it stays.

Moods are generally defined as being either positive or negative, and you will no doubt be used to expressing your own state of mind in terms of being in a good mood or a bad mood (for example, "I've woken in a good mood today," or "That's put me in a bad mood"). Your mood lets you know if something is making you feel good or something is wrong and needs attention.

Rookie Buster

Your mood lets you know if something is making you feel good or something is wrong and needs attention.

Your mood differs from your temperament or personality traits, which are even more general and longer lasting. However, personality traits, such as optimism or pessimism, will tend to predispose you to certain types of moods, and you may find it useful to think about whether you are a "glass half full" or "glass half empty" person.

While your mood is an internal, subjective state that may not affect the specific task you are doing, it can last for hours or days. It can also be picked up and detected by those around you through your posture, the aura you create, or your specific behaviours.

Your mood has an impact on others. If positive, it will create positivity in others. If negative, it will create negativity in others.

Being in control of your mood is essential to good communication. Studies have shown that how well or badly people handle their emotions determines the degree to which others prefer to deal with them. If you can show a degree of consistency of mood, it is much easier for others to deal with you than with someone whose moods swing wildly.

Rookie Buster

Studies have shown that how well or badly people handle their emotions determines the degree to which others prefer to deal with them.

Your physiology

Emotions are vital to the higher levels of human intelligence and performance. Contrary to some popular notions, emotions do not get in the way of rational thinking, but are in fact essential to rationality. However, emotions can impair your rational thinking if you don't have the ability to control or alter your own physiology.

Rookie Buster

Emotions do not get in the way of rational thinking, but are in fact essential to rationality.

Just imagine you are in a very positive frame of mind. You are feeling enthusiastic, motivated and passionate about the project you are working on. Inside your body, energy is moving around freely in a continuous flowing stream, your heart is beating rhythmically, and the electrical signals generated from your heart are smooth, regular and consistent. This is considered an ideal state for clarity of thinking and high level performance, and is referred to as a "state of coherence".

Now imagine you are challenged by someone who doesn't agree with the content of your latest report. You become frustrated by their comments, angry that they could criticize your work and anxious that you may now have to work really late to revise the document. Your

32   negative feelings are now having an impact internally. You can feel the knot in your stomach or perhaps you are getting hot under the collar. Maybe your breath is shortening and your heart is racing. What is clear is that your physiology is changing, and your bodily systems have now moved into a state of chaos. As a result the signals to your brain are impaired and your ability to think clearly, make rational decisions and resolve the issue is affected.

In this instance your emotions have "got in the way". They have upset your physiology, impaired your ability to think rationally and affected your overall performance.

Your ability to sustain a high level of performance is linked to your ability to control or alter your own physiology. So how can you do this? One way would be to learn the techniques in Chapter 3 that will help you to eliminate negative feelings and stop yourself from entering this chaotic zone. However, it is inevitable that situations will occasionally arise when you will find yourself in a state of chaos. One of the quickest ways to return some equilibrium to your bodily systems is to consciously regulate your breathing. You will learn how to do this in Chapter 4.

Your health

Handling your emotions can have consequences for your health and physical wellbeing, both positively and negatively.

For many years, doctors discounted the impact of emotion on health. However, the relatively new science of psychoneuroimmunology shows a biochemical connection between the brain and the immune system that offers a pathway for emotional states to affect health. A Harvard study gives a powerful example of this: 122 men who had suffered their first heart attack were assessed for optimism. Eight years later, of the 25 most pessimistic men, 21 had died; of the 25 most optimistic, just 6 had died.

Evidence is building that suggests the negative emotions of hostility, depression and pessimism can make the body more readily succumb to disease. Disturbing emotions, if prolonged and habitual, may be as strong a medical risk as smoking.

Rookie Buster

Evidence is building that suggests the negative emotions of hostility, depression and pessimism can make the body more readily succumb to disease.

Conversely, in cases of women with breast cancer, the intelligent management of difficult emotions such as anger, sadness, fear and grief has helped the body to fight disease.

All this suggests that you would be wise to manage your emotions well, and to eliminate the negative emotions as much as possible. It is worth bearing in mind that stress is the single largest cause of absenteeism in the UK and is commonly associated with the over stimulus of the hormone cortisol, which is released when the body is in a state of chaos.

Your influence on others around you

You now understand that you should develop the power to control your feelings, to change your moods and even alter your physiology. However, you may not be aware that you also have the power to change the physiology and emotions of others around you.

Rookie Buster

You have the power to change the physiology and emotions of others around you.

Studies have shown that, after just fifteen minutes in conversation, two people with differing bodily rhythms at the start can have very similar physiological profiles by the end.

34   This occurrence is largely due to the open loop design of our emotional or limbic system within our brain. This open loop means that your body transmits signals that can alter the hormone levels, cardiovascular function, sleep rhythm and even the immune function inside the body of others.

By changing the physiology of another person you can also change their emotions. You may have already noticed this yourself. Perhaps you have gone into a meeting feeling down, but after spending half an hour with your upbeat, cheery colleagues, you left feeling a lot better.

People "catch" feelings and moods from others. Our emotions spread like viruses, and good moods, like cheerfulness and warmth, spread most easily. How easily you can pass on your emotional state depends how expressively you convey your feelings through your facial expressions, your voice and your gestures. The more open you are and the better you are at expressing your own enthusiasm, the more readily others will feel the same contagious passion.

Rookie Buster

Our emotions spread like viruses, and good moods, like cheerfulness and warmth, spread most easily.

Moods influence how effectively people work, so if you want to boost co-operation, show fairness and enhance business performance, ensure you are in an upbeat mood.

Laughter is a great signal too. You can be assured that if two people are laughing, it usually means they are on the same wavelength. It sends a reassuring message and can create a chain reaction as it sweeps through a team. You have probably heard the phrase "your smile is your greatest asset". Smiles are the most contagious of all emotional signals. Do a little research yourself: try smiling at someone later today and see just how hard it is for them to resist smiling back.

Getting started

Step 1

Your starting point is to gather data on yourself by completing the EI self-perception questionnaire on the following pages. This data is based on your own perception of your current level of emotional intelligence.

Step 2

Having completed the questionnaire, for each group of five statements, add together the numbers circled and record the total score in the space provided; for example, 2+4+2+3+3 = a total score of 14.

NB: These scores are intended only as an approximate indicator of your level of emotional intelligence, and not an absolute.

Step 3

Take the total score for each element (for example, self-awareness, emotional resilience, and so on), and plot this on to the corresponding blade of the EI Energy Generator on page 39.

As you move through the book and learn more about each of the EI elements, you will be able to re-evaluate your data and identify areas for personal development.

Step 4

You will now be ready to move on to Chapter 3. Here you will gain a greater sense of self-awareness – the most important aspect of EI, and essential for your journey through the book.

Emotional intelligence self-perception questionnaire

Instructions

For each statement, rate yourself on the following scale by circling the appropriate number – for example:

> I am able to recognize my emotions.   1 2 ③ 4 5

When considering each statement, do not spend too long on each one, and imagine yourself in a work context.

1 = Not at all
2 = To a small extent
3 = To some extent
4 = To a great extent
5 = To a very great extent

1. I am able to recognize my emotions.	1 2 3 4 5
2. I stay in control when I am angry.	1 2 3 4 5
3. I am aware of the impact my moods have on other people.	1 2 3 4 5
4. I am able to express my emotions in an appropriate manner.	1 2 3 4 5
5. I am aware of situations that cause me to think negatively.	1 2 3 4 5

TOTAL SCORE: Self-awareness   _____

6. I act decisively when faced with a tough decision, including staff issues.	1 2 3 4 5
7. I am able to perform consistently under pressure.	1 2 3 4 5
8. I am able to press my case in the face of opposition.	1 2 3 4 5
9. I am able to deal with challenge or criticism.	1 2 3 4 5
10. I regulate my work/life balance in order to be resilient.	1 2 3 4 5

TOTAL SCORE: Emotional resilience   _____

11. I have sufficient levels of energy to ensure the
completion of tasks and projects. 1 2 3 4 5
12. I have a positive outlook on life. 1 2 3 4 5
13 I am able to balance my short- and long-term goals
effectively. 1 2 3 4 5
14. I am able to pursue my goals in the face of rejection or
questioning. 1 2 3 4 5
15. I overcome despondency when things go wrong. 1 2 3 4 5

TOTAL SCORE: Motivation _____

16. Before making a decision I listen to the views of others. 1 2 3 4 5
17. I am aware when others are upset. 1 2 3 4 5
18. I am able to put myself in others' shoes and
acknowledge their feelings. 1 2 3 4 5
19. I achieve "buy in" to decisions and ideas for action. 1 2 3 4 5
20. I take into account the input received from others
when making a decision. 1 2 3 4 5

TOTAL SCORE: Interpersonal sensitivity _____

21. I listen to the perspective of others before trying to
persuade them. 1 2 3 4 5
22. I provide a rationale for change when trying to
persuade others. 1 2 3 4 5
23. I find it easy to persuade others to change their
viewpoint. 1 2 3 4 5
24. I receive a positive response to my views on direction
and goals. 1 2 3 4 5
25. I make sure I know where others are coming from
before trying to persuade them. 1 2 3 4 5

TOTAL SCORE: Influence _____

38

26. I make decisions quickly when necessary. 1 2 3 4 5
27. I can make decisions without waiting for all the
   information. 1 2 3 4 5
28. I am prepared to act upon my inner judgement. 1 2 3 4 5
29. I am happy to make decisions even if the given
   information is ambiguous. 1 2 3 4 5
30. I feel comfortable with risk. 1 2 3 4 5

TOTAL SCORE: Intuitiveness _____

31. I adhere to expected standards of personal conduct. 1 2 3 4 5
32. I adhere to prevailing ethical norms when making
   business decisions. 1 2 3 4 5
33. I pursue an ethical solution to a difficult business issue. 1 2 3 4 5
34. I lead by example. 1 2 3 4 5
35. I demonstrate integrity and honesty. 1 2 3 4 5

TOTAL SCORE: Conscientiousness _____

The EI Energy Generator

Your EI Energy Generator comprises seven blades, each one repre-
senting one of the seven elements of the Higgs & Dulewicz EI framework. Each blade is inter-related and of equal importance. By
embracing all the elements simultaneously, you will become a highly
emotionally intelligent individual.

Having now plotted your EI scores, you can see to what extent your
blades are balanced.

The EI Energy Generator is intended to be a motivational tool. You
may be concerned, surprised or pleased by the level of your emotional
intelligence.

Now it's time to identify and commit to the elements you want to
strengthen.

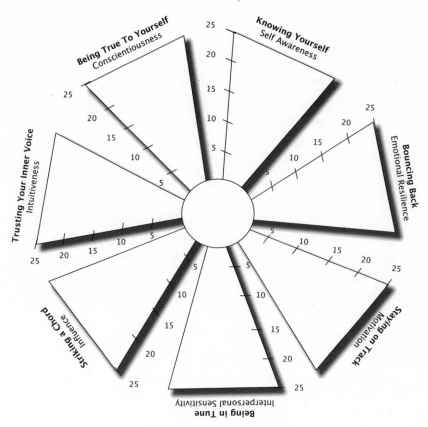

The El Energy Generator

Coach's notes

This chapter illustrates the constant dialogue between your body and your mind, and the holistic nature of emotional intelligence. You will now appreciate that by tuning into your body you can:

- Recognize changes in your physiology.
- Interpret your intuitive feelings.
- Explore your emotional feelings.

By increasing your awareness of what is happening within your body and your mind, and being open and receptive to these inputs, you can control your emotions and alter your physiology to:

- Change the way you feel.
- Influence the way you think.
- Control the way you behave.

This effectively means you can enhance your personal performance, improve your interactions with others and maintain a healthy lifestyle.

Go for it! Having now explored Chapters 1 and 2, you will see the interconnection between the mind and the body. You will recognize that you can join in with this mind/body conversation and really take control of how you feel, think and act.

To act in an emotionally intelligent way, you first need to appreciate what is happening within; what your body is telling you, what you are feeling and how that is influencing the way you behave. To increase this self-awareness, pay deliberate, non-judgemental attention to your thoughts, feelings and body in the "present moment".

By becoming more self-aware, you should find that you can handle those inevitable setbacks more effectively and that you are able to:

- Focus and drive towards your goals.
- Trust your intuitiveness to make decisions.
- Feel comfortable being true to your values and beliefs.
- Find it easier to relate to, work with and influence others.

Self-awareness is the most fundamental element of emotional intelligence. By understanding your emotions and how they affect you, you are in a stronger position to apply the other elements. In fact, it would be fair to say that self-awareness is the very essence of EI.

In Chapter 2 you explored emotions, what they are and where they originate. Now it's time for you to use that understanding to your advantage by applying it directly to yourself.

CHAPTER 3

Knowing yourself

Learning about emotional states

In this chapter you will go on to identify and explore your own emotions and how they affect you on a minute-by-minute, hour-by-hour, day-by-day basis. You will become more aware of how your emotions create the "moods" which you experience, and the impact that these "moods" have on yourself and others.

By regularly assessing what you are feeling, and identifying your mood, you will be in a better position to gauge your emotional "state" and to decide whether it is one that helps you to achieve a positive outcome – or not! If not, you will then be in a position to make a choice as to how you can change it.

Rookie Buster

By regularly assessing what you are feeling, and identifying your mood, you will be in a better position to gauge your emotional "state".

44 By the end of this chapter you will:

- Know just how self-aware you are.
- Understand and recognize both positive and negative emotional states.
- Have a firm belief that you are in control of your emotional state, and that emotional states are changeable.
- Have identified your personal development plan.

With a greater level of self-awareness you'll be more confident, more resourceful and better able to identify and use the appropriate techniques as and when you need them.

What is self-awareness?

Higgs and Dulewicz define self-awareness as: "The awareness of one's own feelings and the capability to recognize and manage these feelings in a way which one feels that one can control. This factor includes a degree of self-belief in one's capability to manage one's emotions and to control their impact in a work environment."

As you know, it is one thing to read and interpret a definition, but it's quite another to understand it and apply it practically in one's life. To do that, you need to take time to consider what is being said and why.

Take a moment here to reflect on this definition.

- What is it saying to you?
- Which are the key words or phrases that stand out?
- Why are they important to you?

It's about knowing yourself

Self-awareness is about knowing what emotions you are feeling at any given time, and being fully aware of how they impact on yourself and others. It's having the ability to "tune in" to your feelings whenever you choose to, and to recognize and understand that your feelings may have changed, and why. And it's about having the ability to be conscious at any time of what you're thinking, how you are feeling and how you are acting.

Rookie Buster

Self-awareness is about knowing what emotions you are feeling at any given time, and being fully aware of how they impact on yourself and others.

Having this level of self-knowledge gives you the ability to manage and control your life and the way you react to people and circumstances, and how you can affect the way others respond to you.

To bring this to life, the following scenario is an example of how someone with low self-awareness might behave...

- *Crash!*
The door is flung open and in crashes one of your colleagues.
- *Wham!*
Their mobile phone is thrown down in a temper on to the desk, just missing the computer screen.
- *Bash!*
They stomp around the room, shouting and cursing at no one in particular.
- *Thump!*
They proceed to throw themselves into their chair and through clenched teeth they start to yell for someone to bring them coffee.

46   Phew! Have you ever experienced something like that? Maybe not exactly that scenario, but at some stage in your life you will have experienced the repercussions of such behaviour. Whilst it may not have been directed at you personally, you would have had a personal reaction to it, to a greater or lesser extent.

Take a moment to think about the impact that this one person's behaviour has had on you or your colleagues.

Firstly, they have disrupted any work in progress simply by crashing into the office. People are automatically thinking "What's wrong? What's up with them?"

Secondly, as the behaviour continues it may start to unsettle others. Some may perceive it as being aggressive and retreat internally, whilst others may be concerned about the distress of their colleague and will want to take action. Perceptions trigger emotions, and these emotions will be unique to each individual.

Replay the scenario in your head once again. Can you see what's happening? Now, *feel* what's happening. Has this feeling changed your mood?

Unease in the office caused by this sort of scenario can lead to a downturn in the overall mood. Your colleague may be totally unaware of the emotional and behavioural impact that they have caused with their outburst, but within minutes the atmosphere within the office has changed and individuals are in a state of emotional turmoil.

Exercise – Impact of behaviour

Think about a time when you have experienced a similar situation, when someone else's behaviour has had a profound impact on you.

Using the prompts on the next page, make some notes, which you can refer back to later.

What was happening?

What were you seeing? What were you hearing?

_____

_____

What were you thinking at the time?
What were you saying to yourself?

_____

_____

How did it make you feel?
What emotions were you experiencing?

_____

_____

How did it make you behave?
Did you remove yourself from the situation? Did you just get on with what you were doing?

_____

_____

Having considered someone else's impact on you, go on to think about a time when your behaviour might have had a significant impact on others. Using the same prompts as before, make a note of your thoughts and feelings.

Then, as a way of starting to open up your own perception, consider this additional prompt:

Were you aware of how others around you were behaving? If so, what were they doing?

48 Personal reflection: Lessons I have learned about myself

Finally take a few minutes to review your responses and identify three key lessons you have learned about yourself, and record them here.

1. _____

2. _____

3. _____

Why is self-awareness important?

Taking time out to reflect on past experiences is one of the key principles of self-awareness, as it provides you with a greater insight into your reactions and responses to people and circumstances. Having a greater level of knowledge about yourself provides you with the platform to progress from, to enhance your own personal performance, and to further improve your relationships with others. You will be more resourceful – in other words, you will have a deeper well of EI that you can draw on at any time.

Rookie Buster

Taking time out to reflect on past experiences is one of the key principles of self-awareness.

By now you may be asking "What else can I do to become even more self-aware?"

In short, the answer is: through analysing yourself more and by asking for feedback from others. This chapter provides you with some practical tools to help you do just that.

What can affect your self-awareness? 49

Your self-awareness can be affected by your *honesty*, your *courage*, your *curiosity* and your *willingness*.

Honesty

You gain a much greater insight if you are honest with yourself about how you think, feel and act. Acknowledge your *true* feelings, even if they are painful. This provides you with "real" evidence for being able to develop your emotional intelligence.

> **Tip:** Take time at the end of the day to sit quietly and reflect on the day's events. Think about what went well; what would you want to do differently if you had that time again, and why? You may wish to record your thoughts in a notebook, which you can look back through later; particular patterns in your behaviour often have a habit of showing up time and time again!

Courage

Your self-awareness can also be affected by how courageous you are in asking for feedback from others. When you receive feedback, you may recognize some aspects of it already; others may surprise you. However, all of it is useful. Without the perception of others, you are never fully aware of your personal impact.

Tip: When gathering feedback, ask for it to be specific. For example, if you want to know how effective you are at listening, ask a colleague before a meeting if they would be willing to observe how you listen, and then ask for their feedback on your effectiveness afterwards.

Curiosity

Having a restless curiosity about yourself and your performance helps you to seek answers as to why things happen, how and why you react the way you do in certain situations, and what you can do to improve yourself.

Tip: Try adopting a state of curiosity at least once a day, asking enquiring questions and being open to the insights these bring.

Willingness

Honesty, courage and curiosity alone are not enough. There also needs to be a willingness on your part to gather information, to learn from it and then to act upon it in order to develop your emotional intelligence.

Tip: Without a willingness to learn, you will never realize your full EI potential.

Exercise – Assessing your willingness to learn 51

Rate your current feelings for these three factors on a scale of 1 to 10;

Energy ☐ | 1 = I'm exhausted.
10 = This is the best I've ever felt.

Openness ☐ | 1 = You'll have to convince me.
10 = I'm excited about new ideas.

Focus ☐ | 1 = My mind is really elsewhere today.
10 = I'm fully focused on what we're here to do.

Multiply the three scores together (energy × openness × focus) and put this total in the box below:

☐

This figure gives your "willingness to learn". The maximum possible score is 1000 (10 × 10 × 10).

So, how willing are you to learn?

To make the most of your learning experience, your rating should be 700 and above.

If it is any lower, identify the possible factors which you think are causing this and consider ways in which you can improve your rating, thereby improving your overall willingness to learn.

If your energy score is low – have a refreshing drink; stand up; move around; get some fresh air; think positive!

If your openness score is low – ask yourself why? What are the reasons for your scepticism or doubt? If this can't be overcome, stop reading this book now, and come back to it when you are in a more receptive state of mind.

52   If your focus score is low – create the right environment. Remove any distractions, both internal and external. (External distractions might include noise, location, comfort; internal ones could be concerns, outstanding actions, etc.)

How does your self-awareness affect others?

Changes in your behaviour are seen and felt by others. But without self-awareness, you won't know how your behaviour may be affecting others. You could unknowingly be having a very negative impact, which will ultimately affect your long-term relationships.

For example, when you are under pressure you may be totally unaware of how you behave. You may become withdrawn, you may start to dictate what has to be done, you may be seen as moody. However you behave, others see and feel the difference.

To raise your awareness you need to know how others see you. With this insight you can change your behaviour and eliminate the negative impact that you have on others.

Tip: Ask others to point out when you are behaving differently. Ask how this is having an impact on them. Share with them how you are feeling, and ask them how they need you to behave to make a positive difference.

Knowing yourself: Bringing self-awareness to life

Your starting point

1. Transfer into this box your self-awareness score from the EI self-perception questionnaire in Chapter 2.

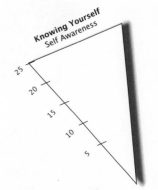

2. Now that you know more about self-awareness, re-evaluate this score and plot it on the Knowing Yourself blade above. This score is an indicator of your level of self-awareness, and is based on your self-perception.

3. Reflect on your entries in your emotions diary (this is fully explained in the next section, "Personal development activities"), and if you recognize there is scope for strengthening your self-awareness, take some time here to jot down your ideas. You may like to think about this in terms of what you could *start*, *stop* and *continue*.

    *   Start – for example, start using positive language to change the way I'm feeling, when I recognize that I am in a "bad" or "sad" mood.
    *   Stop – for example, stop ignoring how my mood is affecting others, and instead ask them for feedback.
    *   Continue – for example, continue asking for more feedback, especially around how my behaviour makes people feel.

4. Use The Johari Window template in the Appendix and consider, in relation to self-awareness, how you behave and how you feel. Jot down your behaviours (in Box 1) and your feelings (in Box 2). A sample of the template is shown here.
    (From Joseph Luft, *Of Human Interaction*, 1969, McGraw-Hill. Material is reproduced with permission of The McGraw-Hill Companies.)

5. Your self-awareness has an impact on others. To gain a true understanding of this, you need to ask others for their feedback. Identify four people who know you well in the workplace and use the five statements from the self-awareness section of the EI questionnaire (page 36 in Chapter 2) as prompts for discussion with each of them. Their perceptions will provide valuable data – some may confirm your own perception, while some may differ.

6. Go back to The Johari Window template, and in Box 1 capture the perceptions shared by you and others. Then complete Box 3 and record anything you had previously been unaware of. The real value of this exercise is in discovering things you don't already know about yourself.

7. Based on your findings, revisit and, if necessary, revise your *start*, *stop* and *continue* actions.

You can now bring your self-awareness to life through the following personal development activities.

Personal development activities

1. Keeping an emotions diary

One of the most powerful ways of raising your self-awareness and gathering information about yourself is to keep an emotions diary. The emotions diary helps you to identify how your emotional intelligence affects you in the workplace.

Invest in a notebook. Use it as your emotions diary. Keep it with you for a two-week period, and use the prompts below to make a note of your feelings in different situations.

Be honest with yourself. This information is invaluable, as it provides you with the "real, live" data which you need as you progress through this book.

My emotions

- Identify the emotion you experienced.
- Describe the situation you were in.
- Identify what triggered the emotion.
- Did you notice how you were feeling or behaving, or did someone comment on your mood/behaviour?
- Record any physiological changes you experienced.
- How long did this emotion last?
- Did you perceive it as a positive or a negative emotion?
- If you perceived your emotion to be negative, how did you deal with it?
- How did you express or communicate your emotion? (For example, by shouting or screaming.)
- What impact did this have on others?
- If you perceived your emotion to be positive, how did you deal with it?
- How did you express or communicate your emotion? (For example, by singing or smiling.)
- What impact did this have on others?

Once you have completed three or four entries, read through them and make a note of any recurring trends or similarities.

If you have identified any specific emotional states, moods, responses and/or feelings that you experience more often than others, make a note of them in your diary.

Then ask yourself "What triggers these?"

56 This will help you to identify any patterns or correlations between your emotional states and their triggers. For instance, is it a particular:

- Person?
- Activity?
- Time? (That "Monday morning" feeling, for example.)

As you move through the book you will find ways to address these emotions and triggers.

2. Becoming more resourceful

An "emotional state" is something that you are experiencing constantly throughout your life. But unlike moods your emotional state doesn't stay around for long.

There are more resourceful, or positive, and less resourceful, or negative, states. A definition of "resourceful" in this context could be "states that help to make your life easy".

Many people think that emotional states are created by situations which you can't control, but it has been proved that you create your own state. This means that you have power to change it whenever you want to. You can move yourself from a less resourceful state to a more resourceful one.

Rookie Buster

Many people think that emotional states are created by situations which you can't control, but it has been proved that you create your own state.

Two of the most powerful ways of achieving a more resourceful state are to change what you actually say to yourself, and to strengthen your positive self-belief.

Your internal chatter

Your internal chatter is the dialogue that you constantly have with yourself, throughout the day.

Stop! Listen! Can you hear it?

Ask yourself, "Is what I'm hearing making me feel positive or negative?"

Some of the conversations that you have with yourself can be very unhelpful, as they generate negative emotions. These emotions then create your mood, and those moods dictate the way you behave. When you are in this state you are more likely to be using very intense language or phrases, such as "I'm really frightened by what they are thinking," "I'm absolutely furious with the way this is going," or "I'm stunned by what's been said."

Simply by changing the intensity of the words or the phrases that you say to yourself can change the impact that they have on your state.

Here are some examples of minimizing your negative impact:

From		*To*
Fearful	➔	Cautious
Furious	➔	Challenged
Stunned	➔	Taken aback

Think about your internal chatter. What negative phrases or words do you hear on a regular basis? Record them in the "From" column below. Then brainstorm some other words which would realistically express how you are feeling, but in a more constructive way, and record them in the "To" column.

From		*To*
_____	➔	_____
_____	➔	_____
_____	➔	_____

58   Here are some examples of maximizing your positive impact:

From		*To*
Enthusiastic	➔	Eager!
Motivated	➔	Excited!
Good	➔	Fabulous!

Now take yourself through the same process as before, but this time looking at increasing the impact of the positive words that you say to yourself.

From		*To*
_____	➔	_____
_____	➔	_____
_____	➔	_____

Now, here's the fun part! Try them out for size. Say them out loud; how do they sound; how do you feel?

Strengthening your self-belief

Self-belief is everything. The loss of self-belief diminishes your self-esteem, self-confidence and ability to remain positive and focused.

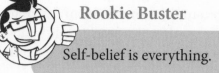

Rookie Buster

Self-belief is everything.

An example of this is what can happen when you are on your way to a business meeting.

You are feeling confident because you are well prepared. You feel positive and, based on your previous experience, you believe that you can have a successful meeting. You start to rehearse the meeting in your mind: you can see yourself and the other person, and you can "hear" what you are saying to each other.

At this stage, you are already anticipating a positive outcome.

However, something starts to happen. You are aware that you are starting to feel uneasy. You're not sure why, but the feeling is definitely there. As you continue on your journey you hear some negative internal chatter creeping in. You start to ask yourself:

- "What if they don't like me?"
- "What if they disagree with my proposal?"
- "What if I don't achieve my objective?"

By this point you are probably beginning to think about the implications of this becoming an unsuccessful meeting, even to the point of believing that you could lose your job over it!

These thoughts appear to come from nowhere, and the trouble begins when you start to believe them. Before you know it, you have gone from a very positive state to a very negative state. You no longer believe in yourself!

You feel worried, demotivated and frustrated, and in only a few minutes you will be walking into the meeting. You try to think more positively, but it doesn't seem to be working. All that you can hear in your mind is "Help!"

What can you do?

You can take yourself around the self-belief cycle, which is illustrated on the next page. This enables you to change the way you are thinking, feeling and behaving, and as a result you are more likely to achieve the outcomes you want.

1. To prevent any negative thoughts and/or doubt in your mind, you need to have a clear objective from the outset.

    Once you have decided your objective, visualize the outcome; imagine how it will feel when you are successful. Store this image in your mind. You can call on it whenever you need to strengthen your self-belief. (This visualization technique is covered in more detail in Chapter 5.)

    Listen to your internal chatter. If it's negative, identify similar situations where you have been successful. Ask yourself, "What went well, and why?" This provides you with evidence to help to keep things in perspective. It creates more balanced thinking.

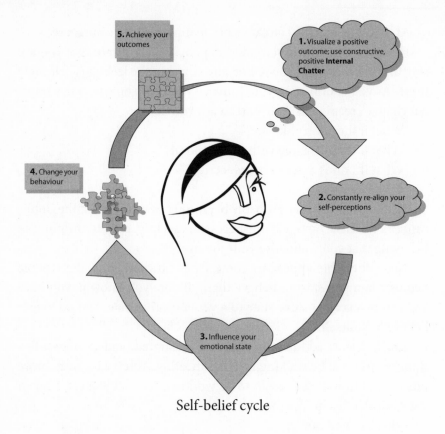

5. Achieve your outcomes

1. Visualize a positive outcome; use constructive, positive **Internal Chatter**

4. Change your behaviour

2. Constantly re-align your self-perceptions

3. Influence your emotional state

Self-belief cycle

Start to think in words and phrases which are more motivational and positive.

Whenever you hear a negative thought, push it away and call upon your past positive evidence to replace it.

2. Perceptions change! Continue to check your perception of the situation. Is anything different which could have caused this change? For example, you may have had some feedback which has caused you to doubt your own ability. If this has happened, find someone whom you trust, and talk it through with them; ask them for feedback; re-align your perception of yourself and the situation.

If you address 1 and 2, you will directly influence your emotional state (stage 3 in the diagram). This in turn will change your behaviour in a positive way, enabling you to achieve your desired outcome (stage 5).

To put this into practice, identify a situation in which your 61
self-belief is called into question. Then take yourself through the
self-belief cycle: make any adjustments necessary; review your
thinking, feeling and behaviour, and acknowledge any effect that
it has.

This is not a technique which brings change about
immediately: you may have to keep coming back to it in order to
make a breakthrough.

Coach's notes

Knowing yourself better helps you to recognize and understand the impact that your emotional state has on yourself and others. It enables you to decide whether the emotional state that you are in is positive and helpful, or negative and therefore unhelpful.

- Without knowing yourself, you can never reach your full emotional intelligence potential. Knowing yourself is at the heart of every EI element.
- Change your mind; change your day! If you recognize that your current mood or emotional state is having a negative impact on yourself and others, choose to do something about it.
- Nothing just happens to you; you are in control. You can help yourself achieve more by changing what you say to yourself, and also by changing what you imagine the end result to be.
- Your beliefs about your experiences and yourself directly affect your behaviour and consequently the impact you have on others.

Go for it! Where better to start your development than with a greater insight into yourself? Make an appointment with yourself and begin to explore what is really going on inside you. When you know what triggers your emotions and how they affect you, you can create a better environment for yourself and those around you. Stop and listen to yourself, and be willing to learn from your discoveries.

Your ability to bounce back from setbacks, cope under pressure and overcome life's ups and downs depends on your level of emotional resilience.

Sometimes you may find yourself more resilient than others, able to pick yourself up, brush yourself off and get on with the task in hand. At other times, things may really get to you. You may feel less able to deal with that cutting comment made by your colleague at the morning meeting. It preys on your mind; you start to feel low, maybe angry or tearful. As a result, you simply can't make decisions or keep focused on what you need to do that day.

This chapter will help you to understand what is happening to you when you don't appear to be strong enough to deal with a situation. It will help you to spot those early warning signals and suggest how you might prepare yourself for those times when you get swept off course.

CHAPTER 4

Bouncing back

What is emotional resilience?

In this chapter you'll read some simple tips that will highlight how your personal attributes, such as self-belief, self-regulation and vulnerability can play an important part in managing yourself and helping you to bounce back.

By the end of the chapter you'll be able to take charge of yourself should you begin to feel emotionally overwhelmed. You will also have the ability to regulate your own physiology through your breathing – one of the most powerful and effective tools you can add to your armoury.

This all means that you will be boosting your emotional resilience. But just what is emotional resilience? Higgs and Dulewicz define it as: "The capability to perform consistently in a range of situations under pressure and to adapt behaviour appropriately. The capability to balance the needs of the situation and task with the needs and concerns of the individuals involved. The capability to retain focus on a course of action or need for results in the face of personal challenge or criticism."

66   Take a moment to reflect on this definition.
- What is it saying to you?
- Which are the key words or phrases that stand out?
- Why are they important to you?

It's about bouncing back

In essence, emotional resilience is about how well you manage your negative emotions when things get tough, and how quickly you can take charge of yourself, refocus on the needs of those around you, and move forward.

Rookie Buster

Emotional resilience is about how well you manage your negative emotions when things get tough.

Take a look at the question below, reflect on the different bullets and, being honest with yourself, consider the meaning of each part and how you would really respond.

Question: When I'm under pressure or things have gone badly wrong, when I've made a big mistake or I've been personally challenged or criticized, do I have the ability to:
- Remain buoyant outwardly and centred inwardly?
- Behave in the way I would normally?
- Produce consistent results and/or show consistency in my performance?
- Think clearly and make appropriate and timely decisions?
- Adapt to the new situation and implement the necessary change?
- Assess the needs of the team and enable them to move on?
- Maintain my self-confidence?

If you can answer a resounding "Yes" to all the above, you probably
have a high level of emotional resilience and have already found ways
to change the way you feel and restore your self-belief in the face of
pressure, following major setbacks or personal challenge.

Now consider the following.

Have I ever:

- Felt downhearted or dispirited when things are difficult?
- Become overwhelmed and felt ineffectual when deadlines are looming?
- Found it tough making timely judgements and decisions when trying to overcome a setback?
- Treated others in an inappropriate manner or found it hard to say the right thing to get the support I need to move on?
- Behaved in a way that was really not constructive or even withdrawn completely under extreme pressure?
- Lost confidence and belief in myself and found it difficult to retain focus and move forward after being challenged or criticized?

If you have never experienced any of the above, then you definitely
have a high level of emotional resilience!

However, it is likely that something in the list resonates with you.
Therefore, you could probably benefit from strengthening your emotional resilience, or at least familiarizing yourself with some techniques
in case you ever feel overwhelmed by your emotions, out of control or
unable to cope.

Avoiding the hijack

Being swamped by your emotions is sometimes called an emotional
hijack. It means that negative feelings such as frustration, anxiety, disappointment, embarrassment, hopelessness, despair, worthlessness,
guilt or uncertainty have completely flooded the emotional brain and
hijacked your attention from the task at hand.

This flood of negative emotions erodes not only your mental abilities (such as your ability to rationalize and make decisions), but also

68   affects your overall emotional intelligence. A downward spiral of self-doubt ensues, and you become unaware of how you are behaving or of the affect you are having on others. Your ability to read the emotions of others is also impaired, and so your interpersonal sensitivity and ability to influence are diminished too.

Why is emotional resilience important?

Disappointments and setbacks are part of everyday life, and mistakes happen – you are human, after all. But how you deal with these in the moment defines the outcome. Being emotionally resilient means you can cope with the inevitable flurry of emotion, while still retaining coherence and clarity of thought and reacting appropriately.

Rookie Buster

Being emotionally resilient means you can cope with the inevitable flurry of emotion, while still retaining coherence and clarity of thought and reacting appropriately.

Saying the wrong thing, or not doing the right thing, can turn a difficult situation into a disaster, and could cost you an important and profitable relationship or even your job.

Low emotional resilience – an example

To bring this to life, let's look at an example of how someone with low emotional resilience might behave.

For the last three months, Phil and his team have been working on a major European conference for one of their key clients. Everyone has put a lot of work and effort into creating an exciting event to meet the client's specific need. This is a big deal financially, and the project is high profile. Phil's team has had some innovative ideas, and all has been going fantastically well.

Phil takes a call from the client. The client explains they have just found out that the venue for the conference has been booked for the wrong dates and there is no availability for the date required. This has huge ramifications in terms of the invited audience, and major financial implications should they have to rearrange the conference. Phil is directly responsible for this error.

How does Phil react?

Phil is devastated and feels confused, helpless, shocked and scared. These feelings well up inside; he feels physically sick, his breathing becomes irregular, and he is unable to function. He recognizes the mistake that he has made and realizes the financial implications for the company. He recognizes that his own credibility has been placed in question and that he might face disciplinary action. The client has demanded to know how such a mistake has taken place. Phil can't explain the mistake; he can hardly speak. He finishes the call abruptly and leaves the building. Totally devastated, he drives home and doesn't reappear the next day.

How does Phil's behaviour impact on his team?

The team learn about the mistake from the client, who is trying desperately to get some answers. They try to call Phil, but he does not respond. They don't know what to do next. The client is furious. The team feel devastated and let down. They are now leaderless. The energy level in the team plummets; they have lost confidence, and are confused and lack direction.

Exercise – Handling the crisis

This scenario highlights the disabling effect that low emotional resilience can have on an individual and also the impact this has on others. Reflect on how Phil handled his emotions, how this affected his behaviour, the impression this made on the client, and the impact on his team. How could Phil have handled this more effectively?

_____

_____

An alternative

When Phil heard the news, he began to feel confused, helpless, shocked and scared as his emotions began to swamp him. Internally, his physiological state went into chaos, his breathing became irregular and he couldn't think clearly or articulate a response. He needed to:

- Take charge of his breathing immediately, and focus on a regular and rhythmic breathing pattern. This enables clearer thinking.
- Find a way to finish the call, and give himself time to address his emotional state. As he would be thinking more clearly because of his regular breathing, he could make an apology, articulate positive action and finish the call: "I can't understand what has happened; I am so sorry. Let me make a couple of calls, find out more and call you back within the hour."
- Take stock; start to rationalize the news and change his emotional state. Draw on a positive state and work through the self-belief

cycle; remind himself of his capabilities and strengths.

- Stop the negative emotions from undermining his confidence or disabling his ability to deal with the situation effectively.
- Be strong and face up to the situation; share the news with a colleague he trusts. Show vulnerability; ask for their help to draw up an immediate action plan; initially verify the situation.
- Address his team; explain; take responsibility and ask for their support to work through immediate actions and find a solution or possible alternatives.
- Prepare what to say to the client; consider "what if?" scenarios; practise aloud or with a colleague. Show professionalism and make the call to the client within the timeframe promised.

How emotionally resilient are you?

Let's stop here and focus on you and how you cope under pressure.

Exercise – Dealing with pressure

Try to recall a work-related situation where you felt under tremendous pressure. Perhaps you were facing a huge setback in a project, addressing a personal mistake, or dealing with a challenging situation.

1. Using the following prompts, take some time to note:
   - The situation or build-up.
   - The people involved.
   - Your thoughts.
   - Your emotional feelings.
   - Your behaviour.
   - How others reacted.
   - The outcome.

   _____

   _____

72   Whether or not you consider you were effective in handling the pressure, reflect on how you could manage your own thoughts, emotional feelings and behaviour if you were facing a similar situation. What would you do differently to help yourself maintain control and ensure you and others continued to perform effectively?

2. Now try to recall any physiological signals (aches, pains, sounds, sensations) that you may have experienced prior to or during the event you have outlined.

_____

_____

Tip: Be alert to your physiological signals in the future – they are your early warning that you are under pressure. Recognize what they are telling you, and take positive action early. Staying in control will help you avoid an emotional hijack.

3. Now, try to recall any intuitive feelings (knowingness or inner voice) that you may have experienced prior to or during the event you have outlined.

_____

_____

Tip: Be open to and value your intuitive feelings – something is resonating with a past experience. Stop and reflect on their meaning. Trust them, and allow yourself to tap into your accumulated life wisdom.

Personal reflection: Lessons I have learned about myself

Finally take a few minutes to draw out three key lessons you have learned about yourself, and record them here.

1. _____

2. _____

3. _____

What can affect your emotional resilience?

Your emotional resilience can be affected if you are:
- Working outside your normal sphere of knowledge and experience.
- Under intense pressure for a prolonged period of time.
- Responsible for a major mistake.

Working outside your normal sphere of knowledge and experience

In such situations you may find that you question your own abilities and feel less confident than you would ordinarily be in your own area of expertise. Self-confidence comes from feeling good about what you do, and knowing you can do the job. If you are outside your comfort zone, it is inevitable you will feel less emotionally resilient, as your self-confidence is not likely to be so strong.

74

Rookie Buster

Self-confidence comes from feeling good about what you do, and knowing you can do the job.

Tip: To boost your self-confidence, reflect on how you felt when you were learning your core skills. Remind yourself that you had the capacity and capability to learn those skills. So with a little time, and being in the right emotional state for learning (see Chapter 3), you will master the new skills or expand the knowledge base that you need for your current role.

Intense pressure for a long time

During periods of intense pressure, it is easy to get locked into the project or task and forget the need for self-regulation. Regulating your sleep, diet, physical exercise and free time are key to maintaining your level of emotional resilience. Let one or all of these slip and you will begin to notice the effect that this has on you. You may become tearful for no apparent reason, or find yourself making little progress with the task.

Tip: To regulate yourself, be conscious of how you are feeling throughout the day, and take action when you feel your concentration is waning or progress is slowing. Be in tune with your bodily needs, and take the time to go for a walk, eat or relax. Simply moving will shift your internal energy, making you feel better and able to think more clearly. The benefit when you return to the task will outweigh the time taken for the break.

Being responsible for a major mistake 75

When the responsibility for a major mistake falls to you, it is likely you will feel overwhelmed by negative feelings. Perhaps you feel guilty, embarrassed, that you have let others down, or that you have failed yourself. Whatever you are feeling will alter your physiology and emotional state and lead to you questioning your belief in yourself. You may find you retreat inwardly, want to spend time on your own and physically remove yourself from the presence of others. These are your signals that your emotional resilience is low and you've lost your self-belief. The earlier you can take positive action the better for you and anyone else involved with you.

Rookie Buster

Regulating your sleep, diet, physical exercise and free time are key to maintaining your level of emotional resilience.

Tip: To regain self-belief, introduce positive self-talk and draw on a more resourceful state. (See the section on personal development activities in Chapter 3.)

How does your emotional resilience affect others?

In Chapter 2, you were introduced to the "open loop" design of our limbic system, and learned that your emotions are contagious. How you feel and the state of your energy will be reflected in those around you.

Let's look at a few examples.

76   Under pressure, a person with *high* emotional resilience will be:
- Calm and collected.
- Consistent in their manner and how they respond to individuals.
- Open to challenge and debate.

They will therefore:
- Create confidence in those around them.
- Retain respect.
- Find others respond well, maintain their focus and perform effectively.

Under pressure, a person with *low* emotional resilience will:
- Appear tense and out of control.
- Show no consistency in what they do or say to others.
- Start to dictate and may bicker about detail.
- Find it difficult to make decisions.
- Appear to have lost confidence.
- Freeze and be unable to react.

They will therefore:
- Lose the confidence of those around them.
- Find the energy level of others will diminish.
- See performance decline in others.

Tip: To strengthen your emotional resilience, be open with those around you and be prepared to show your human side. Acknowledge that you don't handle pressure well and ask others for support. If pressure makes you quiet and withdrawn, let others know that. Ask others to keep a watch for those early warning signals, in case you don't notice. Encourage others to step in when they see these signs and offer their support early.

A note of warning, though. While having a high level of emotional resilience helps maintain a level of consistency in your performance, and creates a confidence in those around you, there is a danger in being *too* emotionally resilient. If you are seen to be too controlled or too regulated from one day to another, and nothing ever seems to affect your outward calm, you could be seen to have lost your human-ness. Being too "in control" of your emotions, you may suppress the energy that is needed to engage and energize others. Too much control may have a negative effect.

Bouncing back: Bringing emotional resilience to life

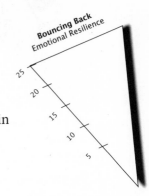

Your starting point

1. Transfer into this box your emotional resilience score from the EI self-perception questionnaire in Chapter 2.

2. Now that you know more about emotional resilience, re-evaluate this score and plot on the Bouncing Back blade above. This score is an indicator of your level of emotional resilience and is based on your self-perception.
3. Reflect on your entries in your emotions diary, and if you recognize there is scope for strengthening your emotional resilience, take some time here to jot down your ideas. You may like to think about this in terms of what you could *start*, *stop* and *continue*.
    *   Start – for example, start removing myself from the situation

78   when I'm beginning to feel wound up.

- Stop – for example, stop taking criticism so personally.
- Continue – for example, continue putting things into context.

4. Use The Johari Window template in the Appendix and consider, in relation to emotional resilience, how you behave and how you feel. Jot down your behaviours (Box 1) and your feelings (Box 2).

5. Your emotional resilience will have an impact on others. To gain a true understanding of this, you need to ask others for their feedback. Identify four people who know you well in the workplace and use the five statements from the emotional resilience section of the EI questionnaire (page 36 in Chapter 2) as prompts for discussion with each of them. Their perceptions will provide valuable data – some may confirm your own perception, while some may differ.

6. Go back to The Johari Window template and in Box 1 capture the perceptions shared by you and others. Then complete Box 3 and record anything you had been previously unaware of. The real value of this exercise is discovering things you don't already know about yourself.

7. Based on your findings, revisit and, if necessary, revise your *start*, *stop* and *continue* actions.

You can now bring your emotional resilience to life through the following personal development activities.

Personal development activities

1. Controlling your breathing

One of the quickest and most effective ways to take control of your physiology is to consciously regulate your breathing pattern. Learning to breathe rhythmically and evenly produces a smooth, regular and stable heart rate, and brings your body into a state of coherence.

If you are in a coherent state physiologically, you will be "in the zone" and able to think, feel and act effectively.

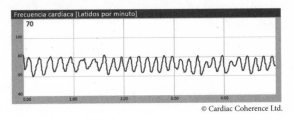

© Cardiac Coherence Ltd.

The smooth, regular pattern generated by the electrical signal of the heart when the body is in a state of coherence

If you are not in the right state physiologically, you will be in a state of chaos, which will inhibit your ability to think, feel and act effectively.

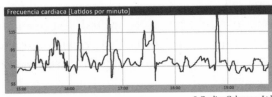

© Cardiac Coherence Ltd.

The sharp, irregular pattern generated by the electrical signal of the heart when the body is in a state of chaos

Rookie Buster

Learning to breathe rhythmically and evenly produces a smooth, regular and repetitive heart signal, and brings your body into a state of coherence.

To take control of your physiology, you will need to breathe rhythmically (which means a fixed ratio of the in to the out breath); breathe evenly (which means creating a smooth flow in and out); and focus on the area of your heart.

Try the following to help with rhythmic breathing:

1. Breathe in to a count of 4.
2. Breathe out to a count of 6.
3. Repeat continually.

To help you remember this exercise, use the acronym BREATHE: **B**reathe **R**hythmically, **E**venly **A**nd **T**hrough the **H**eart **E**veryday.

After a minute or so, you will start to feel a change within yourself and to notice that you are more alert and able to think more clearly.

Initially you may find it easier to close your eyes to practise this technique. Then, when you have mastered that, try with your eyes open.

Practise this technique as often as possible until you can very quickly switch into breathing rhythmically and evenly. Then try it whenever you feel your resilience is being tested – maybe during a difficult telephone call.

If you have to give a presentation and you are struggling with nerves, try using it just before you begin to clear your mind. You might even use it midway through, if you suddenly can't remember what you were about to say!

This technique is very powerful, and once you have mastered it, you can use it anywhere and at any time to take control of what is happening within.

2. Controlling your feelings

To take control of your emotional state, you will need to be really familiar with the characteristics of your feelings and where they reside in your body.

As soon as you begin to feel overwhelmed or swamped by emotion, you will need to be able to *recognize* the feeling and *replace* it with a more positive feeling.

So let's take this step by step.

1. Take a few minutes to jot down the negative feelings that you experience when you are under pressure or facing challenges.

_____

_____

2. Now turn to the "Describing your feelings" exercise in Chapter 2. This asks you to describe the characteristics of positive feelings you regularly experience and identify their movement through the body. If you haven't already tried this, it may be worth completing with your strongest positive feeling.

3. Now that you are familiar with the technique, repeat the exercise for those negative feelings that you have identified above.

4. Next turn to the "Personal development activities" heading in Chapter 3, and find the activity entitled "Becoming more resourceful". Practise this exercise and you'll soon see how quickly you can take control of your emotional feelings.

3. "What if...?" scenario planning

Being prepared mentally, physically and emotionally for everything that you do gives you the confidence and self-belief that you need when things become difficult. Planning and preparation is an activity that is often under-utilized and undervalued, but taking time out to clarify your desired outcome, and to identify the steps you need to take to achieve it, can make you feel more in control.

Rookie Buster

Being prepared mentally, physically and emotionally for everything that you do gives you the confidence and self-belief that you need when things become difficult.

Taking this one step further, spend some time identifying the possible hitches and glitches that could occur – the "what ifs".

Then imagine how you would feel should any of these occur, and what you might say and do. Mentally practise in your head; in the heat of the moment, your brain will follow the pattern practised and help you to stay in control.

Here's an example. Tomorrow you are going to present a proposal to an important client. Think through the things that might happen:

- What if you get held up and are late for the meeting?
- What if your client has to shorten the meeting length?
- What if the "big boss" joins unexpectedly?
- What if your client challenges you on something that is not within your area of expertise?
- What if your proposal doesn't meet the brief?
- What if the client has changed the parameters around what he/she wants?

Now for each possible scenario identify:

- How you might feel.
- What you might say.
- What you might do.

Try to do this exercise before you enter any potentially difficult or challenging situation, and see how much it helps you to remain focused, think clearly and take charge of your emotions.

Coach's notes

Strengthening your emotional resilience will really help you to retain your composure whenever you feel overwhelmed – whether through anger, anxiety or loss of self-belief.

- Boost your self-awareness – understand how you feel and why you react to things as you do.
- Be aware of your physiological signals and listen to your intuitive voice – they are your early warning system.
- Turn on your positive feelings when you recognize the need.
- Don't respond before thinking – allow yourself time to reflect, and have confidence in deferring your response.
- Boost your self-confidence by reflecting on your successes, and identifying what you did each time to make it a success.
- Don't be critical of yourself – accept that you face challenges and will make mistakes. You are human! Share mistakes with others and ask them to help you overcome them and move on.
- Learn to deal with criticism – if you think it is fair, agree and probe for ideas for how to improve. If you don't think it fair, then ask why others hold that view, and be open to feedback.
- Plan in advance, and be prepared for the unexpected.

Go for it! You are now armed with some powerful techniques that will help you to take charge of your feelings whenever you start to feel as though things are getting out of control. By using the breathing technique, you will be able to change your physiological state very quickly, which will enable you to think clearly. You can then concentrate on altering your emotional state to change the way you feel, and control what you say and do.

At first you may need to use these techniques regularly. But as time goes on you will find that you will have strengthened your emotional resilience to a level that no longer requires continual conscious input.

You may then find you can say "Yes" to all those questions posed on page 66!

Notes

Having the drive and determination to achieve what you set out to do; retaining a focus on the goal; maintaining momentum even when things aren't going to plan – all this requires a high level of self-motivation. With a clear and meaningful purpose, a strong sense of self-belief and, most importantly, free flowing energy, you'll be able to stay on track, whatever strays into your path.

By the end of the chapter you will appreciate that your most important resource is your energy. By managing it well you will feel alive and positive about what you are working to achieve; you will be open and willing to find ways around any difficulties and you'll find others inspired to work with you.

CHAPTER 5

Staying on track

What is motivation?

In this chapter you will learn to:
- Plan your day and manage your natural energy reserves.
- Generate positive energy when your reserves are running low.
- Identify what makes you feel good and gives you a sense of fulfilment.
- Overcome distractions and stay present in the moment.

And the key to all this is motivation. But just what is motivation? Higgs and Dulewicz define it as "the drive and energy to achieve clear results and make an impact, and also to balance both short- and long-term goals with a capability to pursue demanding goals in the face of rejection or questioning".

Take a moment to reflect on this definition.
- What is it saying to you?
- Which are the key words or phrases that stand out?
- Why are they important to you?

88 ## It's about staying on track

In essence, motivation is about managing your energy and emotional state to achieve what you set out to do. It relies on your self-awareness in terms of knowing how you feel, whether you are in the right frame of mind for the task in hand, and whether you feel energized to keep moving ahead to get the job done.

Rookie Buster

Motivation is about managing your energy and emotional state to achieve what you set out to do.

Motivation differs from emotional resilience in that your ability to keep going when things get tough is a matter of choice. You can choose to give up if it's too much like hard work, or you can choose to draw on your inner reserves, fire yourself up with incentives and remind yourself of the real purpose and desired outcome.

When your motivation is low, it's usually because your resources are running low, and you'll need to replenish these and generate your own positive energy to move forward.

When your emotional resilience is low, it's usually because you are overwhelmed by anxiety, anger or futility, and are literally disabled by your emotions.

Why is motivation important?

Your motivation and your ability to engage and inspire others is crucial in order to:

- Achieve your defined goals.
- Overcome any obstacles.
- Work with and through others.

Your motivation is underpinned by your energy. Energy levels will ebb and flow, but without energy you won't have the physical strength, mental prowess or the right emotional state to be able to motivate yourself or others.

Rookie Buster

Without energy you won't have the physical strength, mental prowess or the right emotional state to be able to motivate yourself or others.

A highly motivated individual will:
- Show optimism and a positive attitude in the way they behave and the language they use.
- Have high levels of energy and drive.
- Set challenging goals – in both the short and the long term.
- Be focused on performance and achieving the goals.
- Continually look for ways to improve themselves as well as what they do.
- Overcome barriers, obstacles and personal challenge.
- Identify milestones and celebrate those once achieved.
- Engage and inspire belief in others.
- Regularly review their goals as a way of refocusing themselves and re-engaging others.

What can affect your motivation?

Your motivation can be affected by your:
- Energy and drive.
- Goal or purpose.
- Ability to overcome obstacles or distractions.

90 Creating your energy

Knowing where your energy comes from, when your body needs more energy and how you can use your energy most effectively in your daily routine is essential.

Energy can so easily be lost through dissipation, stimulants, tension and emotional or physical excess, as well as prolonged loss of sleep or rest. The more energy that you lose, the more likely it is that you will experience negativity in your thoughts and feelings. This will affect your drive and focus, and ultimately whether or not you reach your desired goal.

Rookie Buster

The more energy that you lose, the more likely it is that you will experience negativity in your thoughts and feelings.

So let's look at your energy sources. Energy comes from:
- Eating – your body gets energy from the breakdown of nutrients like glucose, amino acids and fatty acids.
- Sleeping – your body recharges itself, and the energy absorbed from your food is transferred to your cells.
- Breathing – your body gets the oxygen and energy it requires for life.

Generally you won't notice the accumulation of energy, as this occurs when you sleep. You can however feel and experience the expenditure of energy, and you will know when it needs replenishing through your physiological feelings.

Your bodily signals

Energy is expended not only during physical exertion, but also during mental and emotional exertion.

Your physiological feelings are often associated with your energy levels and bodily needs. When resources are running low or your energy is being drained, your body will indicate this through:

- Hunger.
- Thirst.
- Tiredness.
- Aches and pains.
- Cold and shivering.
- Nervous fluttering in your stomach.

> **Tip:** Food provides the fuel that your body needs, but the energy is only absorbed and transferred during deep sleep. So make sure you are eating nutritional food at regular intervals, drinking plenty to keep your body hydrated, and allowing yourself an average of seven hours' sleep per night.

Managing your energy

If you are providing your body with what it needs, it will create and accumulate energy. Then it's down to you to make the most of what you have, and to use your daily allowance to your advantage.

Let's take a look at some specifics.

Your body-temperature cycle (circadian rhythm)

Your internal body clock governs your daily or circadian rhythm – telling you when to wake and when to feel sleepy. It also controls how deeply you sleep and how long you sleep. This clock is based on your body-temperature cycle. As your body temperature rises, you will feel more awake. As your body temperature drops, you will feel lethargic and tired, and your brain will translate this as meaning that it is time to sleep.

92 **Overcoming your natural dips**

By understanding more about your own body-temperature cycle, you can plan what you do and when you do it. This ensures that you are tackling the toughest jobs when your energy levels are at their highest and you can factor in activities or stimulants that can help you to get over the energy dips.

Rookie Buster

By understanding more about your own body-temperature cycle, you can plan what you do and when you do it.

You probably already know whether you tend to be a morning person (a lark) or a night person (an owl). This will therefore indicate when you have most energy and are at your most productive.

Tip: You will find you will have a natural dip in your energy when your body temperature lowers, at the same time every day. To counter this, you could take a 15–20 minute nap (any longer than 20 minutes and you are in danger of feeling worse). It may be more appropriate to have a cup of coffee or tea, but it will take 20 minutes for this to kick in.

However, if you want to produce your own circadian rhythm chart showing how your body temperature rises and dips over a 24-hour period, log on to http://www.bbc.co.uk/science/humanbody/sleep/crt/.

Knowing when to sleep and wake

Your circadian rhythm chart will also show your natural sleeping and waking pattern, so you can see the best time for you to achieve your quality sleep, when to head to bed and what time to rise. If you can maintain a regular sleeping and waking pattern, you will reap the benefits.

Tip: If you can wake at the same time every day (weekends included), you will find this enhances your energy. And even if you only manage four hours' sleep, but wake at your usual time, you will still feel refreshed and energized.

Your movement

Exercise has many benefits, but in terms of your energy, any movement at all – even using the stairs instead of the elevator, or walking around the building – will help to free any blocked energy and overcome tiredness.

Taking regular physical exercise will of course expend energy, but, through the release of endorphins, oestrogen and thyroxine, you will experience a feel-good factor which elevates your mood and makes you feel more energized. Additionally, other hormones released during exercise improve your ability to unwind and recuperate, resulting in a deeper level of sleep.

Tip: To keep your energy flowing, take a brisk walk as regularly as possible, and particularly after driving.

Your posture

Your posture affects the amount of energy available to you at any time. If your body is in a natural position and your energy pathways are clear, your energy should move throughout your body with ease. However, should it become hindered along its journey, your energy level can drop.

94   Notice your body posture now:

- If it is too relaxed or casual (for example, if you're sitting with your stomach crushed under your chest, or your legs tucked underneath you), you may be trapping or squashing your energy flow.
- If your body is too tense or controlled (for example, if you are holding yourself too upright or rigid), you may not be allowing the energy to enter or flow effectively.

Now centre and align your body, either sitting or standing:

- Feet flat on the floor with a little pressure on the balls of the feet.
- Knees unlocked.
- Hips in alignment with body (not thrust forward).
- Spine upright (not slumped or too rigid).
- Shoulders released and pulled back (not rounded or lifted).
- Head balanced on top of your spine.
- Jaw unclenched.

By sitting or standing up straight your energy flows easily, you feel positive and are able to think more clearly.

Try this quick exercise:

1. Firstly slump your body and observe how it changes your mood.
2. Now sit up, as if there is a piece of string coming out of the top of your head and being pulled up. How do you feel now?

Tip: Make regular checks of your body posture throughout the day, and align and centre as appropriate.

Your physiology and emotional state

You can avoid energy leakage by maintaining a coherent state through your physiology (explored in Chapter 2) and by maintaining a positive emotional state (explored in Chapter 3). Letting chaos reign within, or negative feelings or thoughts pervade, leads to unnecessary expenditure of your energy.

Staying on track requires a positive attitude and the ability to draw   95
on your positive emotional states, such as appreciation, gratitude and
happiness, to maintain coherence as well as momentum.

Defining your goal and purpose

You may have the energy, but if you don't have a clear goal, purpose or
mission, you have nothing to direct that energy towards. Be clear
about what you are trying to achieve, the outcome you desire and how
you will know when you have reached that destination. Identify both
your short- and long-term goals, and ensure that none of your goals
overshadows another.

Rookie Buster

Be clear about what you are trying to achieve, the
outcome you desire and how you will know when you
have reached that destination.

The same applies when balancing your personal goal with your
project/team goal. Both are essential for your motivation, and both
need to be carefully managed.

Knowing your inner driver and what makes you feel good will also
help you to define who and what you need in order to keep you focused
on the outcome.

Identify your main driver now through this simple exercise.

Exercise – What drives me?

You will no doubt be aware of the things that fire you up, give you that
buzz and create your energy, but take a look at the descriptions below
and identify the set of words that best reflects your inner passions.

1. I feel great when I:
   - Outperform others.
   - Meet or surpass my own standards of excellence.
   - Strive to make a unique contribution.
   - Set long-term goals.
   - Overcome challenges.
   - Achieve personal goals.

2. I feel great when I:
   - Am part of a group or team.
   - Am liked and accepted.
   - Can maintain positive interpersonal relationships.
   - Am involved with others in the workplace.
   - Can minimize conflict.

3. I feel great when I:
   - Can exercise influence through my actions.
   - Can arouse strong positive and negative emotions in others.
   - Have a position of power or am known for my reputation.
   - Have control of a situation.

Which set of descriptors most reflects you (1, 2 or 3)? Have a look at the descriptions below – is this what makes you feel good?

1. You are energized by personal achievement, enjoy meeting challenges, love to do well and excel in all that you do.
2. You are motivated by people, prefer to work with others and like harmony in your working relationships.
3. You love to influence others and feel great when recognized for your contribution or your position.

You may find you have one clear set of "feel-good factors", or perhaps a combination of these.

Tip: Reflect on what makes you feel good, and find ways to incorporate these things into your work.
1. Find new opportunities to stretch yourself;
2. Find work and projects in which you are part of a team;
3. Find opportunities to present your ideas.

Overcoming obstacles or distractions

It's very easy to lose your focus or motivation when things are not going quite to plan, when you're distracted by your thoughts or feelings, or when you are "turned off" by others.

You've no doubt experienced a time when you have found it hard to keep focused on the content and direction of a meeting. Perhaps you found a participant's style of delivery difficult to follow, flat or uninteresting. Maybe you didn't believe in the cause or have much belief in the other person. Or perhaps the other person was not factually correct in what they said and you questioned the validity of their input or their integrity.

Any of these, and many other reasons, might cause you to lose concentration, actively "tune out" or disengage. But by being emotionally strong, drawing on your positive energy and thinking about things from a different perspective, your ability to overcome resistance allows you to stay on track and effect a positive outcome.

Tip: Stay "present" at all times, and if you feel you are disengaging, sit up straight with both feet flat on the floor and a little pressure on the balls of your feet, and take a deep, energizing breath. Get involved – ask a question or offer your insight or contribution to the discussion.

98 *How does your motivation affect others?*

As you have seen in Chapter 2, your mood is contagious, and similarly your positive energy and drive will positively affect and inspire others.

To motivate those working with you:

- Involve them in defining the goal, and define the *big* picture.
- Identify each individual's driver or need, and ensure this is met through their role or the job they are doing.
- Be flexible in your approach to addressing their differing needs.
- Apply your senses and your intuitive feelings to tune in to how others are feeling, and respond accordingly.
- Use positive language and act in a way that builds trust and belief in you.
- Build rapport so you are working on the same wavelength (see Chapter 6).

Staying on track: Bringing motivation to life

Your starting point

1. Transfer into this box your motivation score from the EI self-perception questionnaire in Chapter 2.

2. Now that you know more about motivation, re-evaluate this score and plot on the Staying on Track blade above. This score is an indicator of your level of motivation, and is based on your self-perception.

3. Reflect on your entries in your emotions diary, and if you
   recognize there is scope for strengthening your motivation, take
   some time here to jot down your ideas. You may like to think
   about this in terms of what you could *start*, *stop* and *continue*.
   - Start – for example, start recognising when I'm low on energy,
     and take a brisk walk outside.
   - Stop – for example, stop myself from disengaging by forcing
     myself to ask a question.
   - Continue – for example, continue reviewing and revising my goals.
4. Use The Johari Window template in the Appendix and consider,
   in relation to motivation, how you behave and how you feel. Jot
   down your behaviours (Box 1) and your feelings (Box 2).

5. Your motivation will have an impact on others. To gain a true
   understanding of this, you need to ask others for their feedback.
   Identify four people who know you well in the workplace and use
   the five statements from the motivation section of the EI
   questionnaire (page 37 in Chapter 2) as prompts for discussion
   with each of them. Their perceptions will provide valuable data –
   some may confirm your own perception, while some may differ.
6. Go back to The Johari Window template, and in Box 1 capture the
   perceptions shared by you and others. Then complete Box 3 and
   record anything you had previously been unaware of. The real
   value of this exercise is in discovering things you don't already
   know about yourself.

100 7. Based on your findings, revisit and, if necessary, revise your *start*, *stop* and *continue* actions.

You can now bring your motivation to life through the following personal development activities.

Personal development activities

1. Harnessing your energy

You will know that there are some things and some people that make you feel good. It's almost as if they switch you on, and suddenly you feel full of energy, full of passion and ready to surge ahead.

Knowing what those things are and who those people are is important to keep you motivated towards your goal.

Step 1
Reflect on the list below, and if you believe these are your energy givers, identify who is involved, what you are doing and how often you are consciously tapping into this to top yourself up.

Activity	*Who/What/How often*
• Humour and laughter	
• Optimists, positive people	
• Time alone	
• Social activities	
• Self-development	
• Personal interest/passion	
• Music	

Consider:
- Whether you are giving yourself enough exposure to your energy givers in a normal working week.
- The people you work with, and identify who you work with best to achieve what you need to achieve.
- Minimizing the time spent with people who drain your energy.

- Your own preference for being/working alone and for being/ working with others.

Step 2
Now take a look at the two sets of descriptors below and tick the words that most reflect you:

Set A
- Attuned to the external environment.
- Prefer to communicate by talking.
- Work out ideas by talking them through.
- Learn best through doing and discussing.
- Have broad interests.
- Sociable and expressive.
- Readily take initiative in work and relationships.

Set B
- Drawn to the inner world.
- Prefer to communicate in writing.
- Work out ideas by reflecting on them.
- Learn best by reflection and mental "practice".
- Focus in depth on my interests.
- Private and contained.
- Take initiative when the situation or issue is very important to me.

In which set did you tick the most descriptors – A or B?

If A, you are more likely to draw your energy from other people and activity. You will probably direct your energy and attention outwards, and receive energy from interacting with others and from taking action.

If B, you are more likely to draw your energy from within – your own ideas and experiences. You will probably direct your energy and attention inwards, and receive energy from reflecting on your thoughts, memories and feelings.

102   2. Visualizing your goal

Visualization can really bring your goal or purpose to life, by creating a powerful mental image of exactly what you will see, hear and feel once you have achieved your goal.

Picture the scene, complete with images, of your future desired outcome, and step into that feeling. Try to create the detail: in pictures, feelings, sounds and smell.

By repeating this exercise regularly, you embed that desired outcome in your subconscious mind, and subsequently create the motivation that you require to work towards it.

3. Eliminating distracting thoughts

When concentrating on a particular task, keep focused on the present moment at all times. Anything else that enters your mind is a potential distracter and needs to be removed.

To remove these thoughts or interferences, simply take a sheet of paper and jot down what they are and when you will deal with them. By jotting them down, you don't have to worry that you may forget to address them – after all, you have now recorded them. And by allocating a specific time, you have committed to deal with them. You can now return to the task in hand.

Should the thought re-enter your head, push it out immediately, emphasizing when you will take action – for example, "I am going to make that call at lunchtime today."

Initially, you may have to repeat this exercise several times, but the more you use the technique, the quicker your mind accepts this methodology. However, be aware your mind does not accept this technique if you don't action what you agreed to.

Coach's notes

Using your energy effectively will really help you to remain motivated, to focus on your desired outcome and to overcome any obstacles.

- Know your daily energy pattern and use this to your advantage.
- Identify your energy givers and build them into your day and week.
- Practise optimism, but be realistic.
- Watch your language; turn a negative comment or a criticism into a positive opportunity.
- Define your short-term goal and overall purpose and make these clear, meaningful and inspiring.
- Identify milestones and celebrate when you reach them.
- View obstacles as challenges and reframe the situation to see it from another perspective.
- Notice when you become distracted or disengaged, and do something about it.

Go for it! Now you know what makes you feel good and you can generate positive energy. Clarify what you want to achieve, set specific goals, manage your energy and GO FOR IT!

Notes

Your ability to "tune in" to other people and to recognize and understand what's going on inside them and between you, on a "feelings"
level, is determined by your interpersonal sensitivity. By building your
interpersonal intelligence, and by being open to and valuing the input
of others, you can build "great" relationships which are both empathetic and harmonious.

CHAPTER 6

Being in tune

Great relationships

Great relationships are those where you:

- Feel that you really connect with the other person.
- Really understand each other's thoughts and feelings.
- Respect others' views and concerns and accept that they are relevant and valuable.
- Are sensitive to each other's needs.
- Both truly value your relationship and its mutual benefits and rewards.

These relationships can only exist where there is empathy between you, where you have a high regard and respect for each other and most importantly where there is trust. It's about establishing rapport.

The good news is that some of these relationships already exist in your business life. You will recognize them as the ones in which you can challenge each other without conflict. Where you support each other's ideas and have shared commitment to the outcomes that you are both working towards. These are the relationships where you both feel valued.

108   This chapter explores your interpersonal sensitivity in terms of establishing rapport and building trust.

By further developing your active listening and questioning skills, you will be able to create an empathetic climate where others feel encouraged to talk to you and that it is "safe" to do so.

In Chapter 3 you focused on self-awareness. Now it's time to put yourself in the other person's shoes and consider everything from their perspective: how they are feeling, what their needs are, and how you can address them. In short, this chapter is about developing your *other* awareness.

It is also a precursor to the next chapter, "Striking a Chord".

What is interpersonal sensitivity?

Higgs and Dulewicz's definition is:

"The ability to be aware of, and take account of, the needs and perceptions of others when arriving at decisions and proposing solutions to problems and challenges. The capability to build from this awareness, and achieve the commitment of others to decisions and action ideas. The willingness to keep open one's thoughts on possible solutions to problems and to actively listen to, and reflect on, the reactions and inputs of others."

Take a moment to reflect on this definition.

- What is it saying to you?
- Which are the key words or phrases that stand out?
- Why are they important to you?

It's about being in tune   109

Ultimately it's about building and sustaining long-term, mutually rewarding relationships with others.

An emotionally intelligent way of achieving this is by developing your interpersonal sensitivity. It's being able to communicate with others on an empathetic level. It's about stepping into the other person's shoes, not just on a thinking level but on a feelings level as well.

By picking up and tuning in to both the verbal and non-verbal signals from the other person, you will develop an invaluable insight into their perspective.

Why is interpersonal sensitivity important?

Being interpersonally sensitive when communicating with others provides a quality and richness to the information which is being shared. This information is based on both fact and feelings.

Inviting others to share and being open and non-judgemental increases the value of your discussions. It also raises everyone's willingness to be open, builds trust and creates an environment in which people are supportive towards each other and each other's ideas.

Rookie Buster

Inviting others to share and being open and non-judgemental increases the value of your discussions.

This in turn creates an inclusive relationship, where everyone shares decision-making, responsibility and ownership.

110 *What can affect your interpersonal sensitivity?*

Your interpersonal sensitivity can be affected by your ability to establish rapport with others. If you can understand what it takes to establish and maintain rapport, and then apply it to all of your associations, in business and otherwise, you will develop extremely valuable and rewarding relationships.

Establishing rapport

Rapport is about having a quality of mutual influence and respect between you and others. It is created when you:
- "Get along" with someone.
- Feel a true "connection" with them.
- Both understand each other's perspective.
- Are willing to listen to each other without judgement.
- Can both share your thoughts and feelings without feeling vulnerable.

Exercise – Who do you have rapport with, and why?

Think of someone with whom you feel this sort of connection.

Using the following prompts, make a note of the reasons why you think this connection exists.
- What qualities does the other person have that you value in your communication with him/her?

_____

_____

- How do you feel during and after the time that you have spent with him/her?

  _____

  _____

- What makes this a "great relationship"?

  _____

  _____

Take a moment to reflect on your responses, and then ask yourself, "If they were to complete the same exercise, what would they think, feel and say about me?"

_____

_____

Personal reflection: Lessons I have learned about myself

Finally take a few minutes to draw out three key lessons you have learned about yourself, and record them here.

1. _____

2. _____

3. _____

An underlying principle in establishing rapport is to have respect for one another. Having respect for someone means to treat them with consideration. It also means regarding them for who they are and

112 accepting and valuing their unique way of perceiving things.

Your interpersonal sensitivity can also be affected by your ability to create and build trust within a relationship.

Building trust

Trust is a major factor in any relationship. In fact, without trust there is no relationship. It is developed over time and requires a certain amount of risk taking and testing.

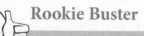

Rookie Buster

Without trust there is no relationship.

Trust is a very precious commodity, and once established it must be nurtured and handled with care.

There are four key principles of trust: it doesn't just happen, it grows; it's both rational and emotional; it has to be two-way; and it's personal.

Trust grows, it doesn't just happen
Trust is something that grows and develops over time. You can't simply demand it, as it has to be earned and deserved. This can be done in a number of ways – for example, demonstrating that you do what you say you will, (see Chapter 9, Being True To Yourself), recommendation by a third party, and evidence of past performance.

Trust is both rational and emotional

On the rational side, trust is developed in others through your knowledge, expertise and experience. This establishes your credibility. Your credibility is established not only through your business expertise, but also through your "presence"; how you look, act, react and talk about your subject.

On the emotional side, it is developed through your support and concern for the other person's needs. This establishes intimacy. In an emotional intelligence context, intimacy is about making a connection with the emotional state of the other person.

Trust has to be two-way

Trust is a two-way thing! You can love, hate, or respect someone else without them thinking the same way about you, but you can't expect the same with trust. For trust to exist in a relationship it has to be reciprocal.

> **Tip:** Trust is dynamic. Don't take it for granted! To gain and sustain trust takes forever, but to lose it takes only a moment. Constantly review the trust level within the relationship using your communication and intuitive skills, and where necessary take appropriate action to boost it.

Trust is personal

People don't trust organizations; they trust people.

People trust the reputation of an organization because of the quality of their product and the services of their people. But everything comes down to the quality of the relationships that clients have with the people in the organization; not the product itself.

114 *Developing an empathetic climate*

To be able to create rapport and trust in a relationship, you need to develop an empathetic climate, in which people feel valued for saying what they really think, feel and believe, and can do so without any fear of criticism, judgement or punishment.

Your interpersonal sensitivity is therefore critical in creating this climate and requires you to:

- Listen to what is being said.
- Use empathy to clarify your understanding of the meaning behind the words.
- Ask great questions to get to the heart of the matter.

Now it's time to explore these elements further.

Listening actively

Listening is an active process that not only enables us to acquire information, but also helps us to empathize, evaluate, acknowledge and appreciate others. We spend much of our time listening, yet it's not very often that we consider how good our listening skills are and what improvements we need to make.

It is an activity that most of us take for granted. However, bad listening can have a significant negative impact on relationships with others, and good listening is an ingredient that others will value highly.

Rookie Buster

Bad listening can have a significant negative impact on relationships with others.

So here are a few tips for building on your listening skills.

Be receptive and pay attention   115

This deliberate action is intended to demonstrate a willingness to listen to the other person. Whether you say it or think it, "Tell me more" is the key to success. If you hear yourself saying to yourself "I wish he/she would shut up," then you will unconsciously be communicating this very desire. The other person will shut up and be left with the feeling that you are not interested in his/her responses.

Exercise – Listening: more or less?

Over the next couple of weeks, observe people in internal meetings at work.

Notice those colleagues who:
- Do a lot of talking.
- Do a lot of listening.
- Talk loudly in order to be heard.
- Interrupt a lot of the time.

Then consider the impact that their behaviour has on the other participants, and the effect of the meetings and their overall success.

Use silence appropriately

The other person needs the opportunity and space to be able to speak. A simple rule to remember is that if you are speaking, the other person is not!

Rookie Buster

A simple rule to remember is that if you are speaking, the other person is not!

In a face-to-face situation, using non-verbal cues such as nods and eye contact will show that you are listening. Similarly, using "Yes" and "I see" and "Really?" will show that you are listening.

116   Remove distractions

Removing distractions is important if you are to respond quickly and accurately to the other person's needs. This includes physical distractions, such as noise and the environment, although these may be out of your control.

But the main thing that you can control is mental distraction – in other words, day-dreaming or thinking about other issues or worries, or rehearsing your response to them.

It is possible to contain and minimize any of these mental distractions. For example, some of your most intrusive thoughts can be categorized into three types:

- Problems that haven't been resolved.
- Problems that can't be resolved.
- Things to remember.

For unresolved problems, ask yourself "When do I need to attend to this?" If the answer is now – deal with it before the meeting. If you can't do that, you have to mentally "shelve" it – store it away for later.

If the problem is non-resolvable, the most likely reason for these thoughts creeping into your mind is that they are important to you. You need to be disciplined with yourself and stop these thoughts when they creep into your mind at the wrong time – remain focused. Also make sure that you find somewhere appropriate to talk and think about the problem, possibly using your support network.

Finally, if you are thinking about something so that you don't forget it, write it on a Post-it note and stick it somewhere you can't miss it!

Be patient

If the other person has had the chance to complete what he/she wanted to say, they will find it easier to relax and listen to you attentively. Avoid speaking over them or finishing their sentences. Patience can not only aid understanding, but in some instances it can prevent a conversation deteriorating into a potential misunderstanding.

Clarifying understanding 117

Reflecting
Reflecting is a valuable communication skill that can be used in many situations. What is the value of reflection?

To the other person, it:
- Confirms that they are being listened to, understood and accepted on their own terms.
- Gives them an opportunity to correct any misunderstandings.
- Helps to clarify the situation from their perspective.

To you, it:
- Helps to separate information into manageable chunks.
- Helps to provide a breathing and thinking space by creating a pause in the flow of information.
- Helps to check out whether you are understanding the information you are receiving, both rational and emotional.

How is this done?

Simple restatement
This is saying back to the other person what he/she has told you (sometimes known as "parroting"). You can restate by repeating, in reflective tones, the last few words they have said. For example: "So – what you've said is, you're feeling nervous because you've got to make the presentation."

Paraphrasing the essentials
This gives you the chance to highlight key points made by the other person, in your own words. For example: "Let me just check I've got this clear in my mind; what you are really saying is …"

Summarizing
Summarizing is a technique similar to reflection that enables you to communicate to the other person that you have understood what they have told you, and to clarify what has been said. Used near the end of

118   a conversation it is a helpful recap for you and them, and minimizes the risk of misunderstandings. Summarizing before ending a conversation is a valuable habit to get into. For example: "Let's take a moment to recap the main points so far …"

Rookie Buster

Summarizing before ending a conversation is a valuable habit to get into.

Asking great questions

Another vital technique to develop alongside your listening skills is questioning. Questioning and listening can be seen as two sides of the same coin. A conversation is built around asking questions and listening attentively to the response.

You will know from your personal experience that it is fairly easy asking somebody what they *think* about a situation or a solution, but less so asking them how they *feel* about it. This is because thinking is based on fact and general information, which is common to all and exists outside the "self", whereas feelings are unique to each person, and represent our inner "self".

So in order to enable the other person to tell you how they think *and* feel, you have to ask the "right" questions.

There are numerous types of questions which you can ask, but in the context of this chapter the following seven different categories of "great questions" will be the most helpful. By asking a great question you can clarify and discover information on a different level; you can begin to exchange both facts and feelings.

1. **Anticipation**
   - "What might happen?"
   - "What if it doesn't work out the way you want it to?"
   - "What's your back-up plan?"

2. **Assessment**
   - "What do you think is best?"
   - "How does it look to you?"
   - "How do you feel about it?"

3. **Clarification**
   - "What do you mean?"
   - "What does it feel like?"
   - "What do you want?"

4. **Evaluation**
   - "In what way?"
   - "Is it good or bad?"
   - "What do you think it means?"

5. **Exploration**
   - "What are your other options?"
   - "Shall we brainstorm that?"
   - "Can we explore that some more?"

6. **Example**
   - "What would it look like?"
   - "What would it feel like?"
   - "Such as?"

7. **Elaboration**
   - "Can you tell me more?"
   - "What other ideas/feelings do you have?"
   - "What else?"

120

> **Tip:** One of the best ways of seeing this in action is to critique different types of television programmes, for example soap operas, chat shows, current affairs, and even *Big Brother*. Listen to the types of questions that are asked. Watch the reaction and response that others have to the questions, and evaluate the level of rapport between people. Once you have established rapport and built trust, others become more willing to engage with you and to share both their thoughts and feelings.

How does your interpersonal sensitivity affect others?

Your interpersonal sensitivity enables others to feel valued and sup-ported by you.

Having this understanding on an "intimate" level develops a rela-tionship in which you are both willing to listen to and consider each other's point of view and to be open to all ideas and opinions, in order to come to a mutually rewarding outcome or solution.

Being in tune: Bringing interpersonal sensitivity to life

Your starting point

1. Transfer into this box your interpersonal sensitivity score from the EI self-perception questionnaire in Chapter 2.

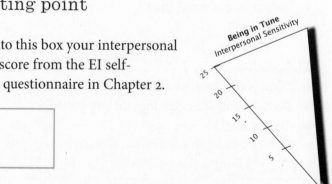

2. Now that you know more about interpersonal sensitivity, re-evaluate this score and plot on the Being In Tune blade opposite. This score is an indicator of your level of interpersonal sensitivity, and is based on your self-perception.

3. Reflect on your entries in your emotions diary, and if you recognize there is scope for strengthening your interpersonal sensitivity, take some time here to jot down your ideas. You may like to think about this in terms of what you could *start*, *stop* and *continue*.

   - Start – for example, start sharing my thoughts and feelings with others in order to demonstrate trust.
   - Stop – for example, stop interrupting people when they are speaking.
   - Continue – for example, continue getting feedback on how well I'm able to put myself in other people's shoes.

4. Use The Johari Window template in the Appendix and consider, in relation to interpersonal sensitivity, how you behave and how you feel. Jot down your behaviours (Box 1) and your feelings (Box 2).

5. Your interpersonal sensitivity has an impact on others. To gain a true understanding of this, you need to ask others for their feedback. Identify four people who know you well in the workplace and use the five statements from the interpersonal sensitivity section of the EI questionnaire (page 37 in Chapter 2) as prompts for discussion with each of them. Their perceptions

122

will provide valuable data – some may confirm your own perception, while some may differ.

6. Go back to The Johari Window template and in Box 1 capture the perceptions shared by you and others. Then complete Box 3 and record anything you had previously been unaware of. The real value of this exercise is discovering things you don't already know about yourself.

7. Based on your findings, revisit and, if necessary, revise your *start*, *stop* and *continue* actions.

You can now bring your interpersonal sensitivity to life through the following personal development activities.

Personal development activity

Establishing rapport through communication

We have seen that it is much easier to ask somebody what they think, but less so to ask them how they feel. So in order to enable others to share their innermost feelings, it is necessary first to develop trust.

Consider why it is important to share feelings. What value does it bring to your relationship?

If it's important to find out how somebody feels, why can't you just go ahead and ask them? The answer is that you can, but only once you have established rapport and built trust; once there is mutual respect and openness.

For someone to share their thoughts and feelings with you, they have to take a risk; a risk in making themselves vulnerable. By disclosing their feelings to you, they will naturally perceive that you have a level of power which could be used to betray or undermine them. They have to be able to trust that this isn't going to happen.

As you have already seen, one of the main ways of creating trust is through communication. By listening actively, questioning and clarifying for understanding, you create an empathetic environment in which both parties take risks when sharing thoughts and feelings. This in itself builds trust, and as a result the payoff in the quality of the outcomes and the long-term relationship is fantastic!

Rookie Buster

One of the main ways of creating trust is through communication.

The more of yourself you invest, the more the other person invests of themselves as well.

To illustrate this, imagine yourself at an informal business gathering. You are on your own, and your boss has told you that it is important that you network, so you need to identify and establish some quality business contacts – and off you go.

You pick up a drink and introduce yourself to a likely looking candidate. Within minutes of starting the conversation you sense that this conversation isn't going anywhere, especially not towards becoming a useful contact! You feel a strong urge to find someone else more interesting and more engaging.

You stop listening to what they are saying and you look around the room (subtly) to spot your next candidate.

This cycle may happen two or three times until you come across somebody who seems to be "like minded", who is "on your wavelength" and whom you find easy to "tune in to".

You both seem very happy and comfortable with each other and the time you spend with them is far more enjoyable and satisfying because you both feel that you have connected with each other.

Finally, you have to finish the conversation and leave, but before you do you exchange business cards and agree to phone to arrange a further meeting. You both walk away – smiling!

The following model demonstrates how this is achieved by considering the levels of communication required when building rapport.

This exercise will help you to:

124
- Understand what takes place at each level of the conversation.
- Identify which level you are at.
- Prepare appropriate questions which will move the conversation up the levels.

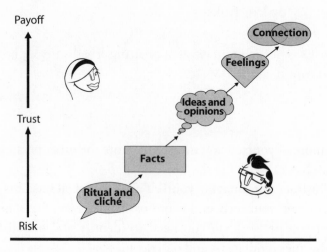

Establishing rapport through communication

Very low risk – very low trust – very low payoff

For example: "Nice to meet you." "Isn't the weather lovely?"

This is the most basic exchange of information.

This exchange usually happens immediately before or after an introduction. It is necessary as it establishes social contact and etiquette. The topic of conversation is considered very safe and any questions asked are either rhetorical or only require one-word answers.

There is very little risk of exposing one's feelings at this level, therefore there is little need for any trust, and as a result the exchange doesn't provide any insight to the other person. This stage only takes a matter of seconds before moving on to the next level.

Facts

Low risk – low trust – low payoff

For example: "Which office/branch do you work in?" "What do you do?"

This is where you start to collect data about each other, all of which is factual. It helps you to develop a picture of each other's world.

Even though the information is impersonal, you begin to form a view of each other based on your feelings and what you are sensing; whether you like each other or not; whether you wish to continue talking to each other; whether there is any value in taking this conversation further. At this stage you also tune in to your own feelings and become more aware of them.

You may start to establish some common ground by uncovering some shared experience or contacts.

Taking the earlier scenario as an example, this is probably the level that the first few interactions would have got to. They became unsatisfying because there wasn't enough common ground for you to develop the conversation. In fact it would have dried up. People are social creatures and need to have stimulating interaction with others.

In order to do that, you need to move up to the next level.

Ideas and opinions

Medium risk – medium trust – medium payoff

For example: "That's interesting, what do you think about that?" "Do you think that's a good/bad idea?" "It appears to me …"

At this level the information which you share is about personal views and opinions as opposed to common thinking. Here you are able to ask for each other's opinions without any threat, because you have already built sufficient trust to do so.

Asking for and exchanging information at this level demonstrates that both parties want to have a better understanding of the other's perception in order to influence and share the outcome.

126   This is when you start to feel that the conversation develops its own momentum.

You may establish agreement to your proposed ideas and solutions, but this is only on a rational level. In order to really establish buy-in and share the outcome you have to be communicating on a feelings level as well.

High risk – high trust – high payoff

For example: "How do you feel about that?" "If I were in your shoes, I would probably feel…" "It feels like the right way forward – do you agree?"

Communicating at this level allows you to tune in to the other person's emotional state and enables you to empathize and support them appropriately. In a business context, this would be working in true partnership. It is about having respect for what each person needs and ensuring, wherever possible, that you can support each other in achieving those needs.

To encourage others to share their feelings, see the feelings-based conversation activity in Chapter 7.

Finally, the highest level of rapport is connection.

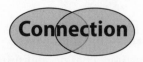

Very high risk – very high trust – very high payoff

For example: "I know exactly what you're thinking!" "I know that you're feeling …"

This is the ultimate level of rapport, at which you can anticipate exactly how the other person thinks and feels. It feels instinctive.

You may even hear yourself using phrases like "We're really on the same wavelength now," and "We're able to see eye to eye on this one."

Be warned, though. The connection level is not achieved with everyone, and it has to develop over time. It is most likely to be achieved with family members, your partner, best friend, a close confidant, or a long-term colleague. You may never achieve it with a client. Don't be disappointed though – if you remain interpersonally sensitive to this fact and are able to communicate at a feelings level whenever it is appropriate, that is enough!

Putting the model into practice

Step 1
To bring this model to life, think of a current relationship in which you would like to further develop rapport.

Make a note of it here, with your reasons for wanting to improve it – for example, "So that I can really understand the difficulties he has with making a commitment to my solution. What are his real concerns? Why isn't he comfortable with my proposal?"

Step 2
Referring to the model, identify which communication level you spend most of your time on with this person and why you think/feel that is. For example: "Facts. I get the impression that he doesn't want to be disloyal to his colleagues."

---

128 **Step 3**

Now set yourself a target for your next conversation or meeting with them. For example: "By the end of the meeting I want him to feel able to speak to me in confidence about his real concerns. Therefore I need to be communicating with him at the 'feelings' level."

_____

_____

_____

Step 4

Whichever level you have identified as your goal, you can now go on to prepare some "great questions" which will help you reach it.

Using the question types provided earlier in this chapter, make a note of some useful questions which you can use during your conversation. Make them relevant to your personal situation, and put them into your own words.

_____

_____

_____

Step 5

Then try them out for size! Say them out loud. Find a colleague and ask him or her to role play your conversation.

- How do your questions sound?
- Will they get you the information that you want/need?
- What would you be thinking/feeling if you were in their shoes?
- How can you disclose how you feel? What words can you use to demonstrate empathy?

Make any changes necessary.

But a word of warning! You *must* listen. The danger with preparing questions in advance is that you can be too focused on your next question, and not be listening to the other person's responses.

Rookie Buster

The danger with preparing questions in advance is that you can be too focused on your next question, and not be listening to the other person's responses.

The quality of the questioning is in the listening, and vice versa. Make sure that you employ all of your listening skills, especially the summary and clarifying techniques, to check understanding.

Finally, spend time immediately after your conversation or meeting to review your goal. Did you achieve it?

Consider the following prompts:

- Did you achieve the level of communication and understanding that you wanted?
- How did you feel during the conversation?
- What were you thinking?
- How effective was your questioning technique?
- How well did you listen?
- To what extent do you feel satisfied with the outcome?

This is a dynamic process. Every time you have a conversation with somebody, whether it is a new or long-standing relationship, you both automatically start at the ritual cliché level. However, where you already have rapport you move very quickly up to feelings. Just think for a moment how valuable this is in terms of your interpersonal sensitivity.

Coach's notes

Improving your interpersonal sensitivity helps you to communicate with people on an empathetic level. By creating an emotional climate in which thoughts and feelings can be shared in a respectful and considered way, you will be able to fully understand and appreciate each other's perspectives.

Establishing this level of understanding then provides you with an insight into how the other person is making their decisions and how receptive they are towards your ideas, etc.

So, to keep this level of interpersonal sensitivity you must bear the following points in mind:

- Always "tune in" to the thoughts and feelings of others. Be on their wavelength!
- Continue to strive to see the situation from the other person's perspective, and be willing to take their views and needs into account.
- Value the quality of information that someone else is willing to share with you.
- Respect is an important factor within rapport. You must always treat the other person's thoughts and feelings with consideration.
- You are only ever a custodian of trust. It is a quality which is bestowed on you by the other person's perception of you. If you break the trust, you can very rarely repair it.
- Remember to create and nurture an empathetic climate by asking appropriate questions, listening actively and clarifying your understanding.

Go for it! Using your interpersonal sensitivity on your EI journey, you are in a stronger position to encourage others to come with you. A wonderful Native American proverb brings this to life: "When seeing the world from another man's eyes, you must first step into his moccasins. But to truly understand what he sees and how he feels, you must then walk two moons in them!"

Influencing is only possible with a high level of interpersonal sensitivity. Building on the elements you explored in Chapter 6, this chapter highlights the attributes needed to become an inspirational person; a person who naturally influences through their genuine respect and regard for others.

In this chapter you will explore the use of language and behaviour in:

- Expressing yourself emotionally.
- Widening your views and perspectives.
- Building confidence in others.
- Gaining respect.
- Encouraging feelings-based conversation.

CHAPTER 7

Striking a chord

How influence can happen

Influencing others can happen without you even knowing. You arrive at work in a bubbly, light-hearted mood. You're really excited about a new project. You call your team together and enthusiastically talk it through, setting out the key activities and the timeline. Your mood, your quickness of pace, the excitement in your voice and your confident language soon engage the team, and before the meeting finishes they are fired up and raring to go too.

This came naturally, you were genuinely enthused and energized, and with the help of the open loop system discussed in Chapter 2 you "infected" and influenced the others.

However, circumstances could have been very different. You could have been kicking off a new project which you didn't really believe in, and at a time when the team already had a very heavy workload. Then you would have needed to be more considered in your style, language and approach, more attuned to the feelings and differences of the individuals, more enabling in achieving the desired outcome and in striking a chord.

134 *What is influence?*

Here is how Higgs and Dulewicz define influence: "The capability to persuade others to change a viewpoint based on the understanding of their position and the recognition of the need to listen to this perspective and to provide a rationale for change."

Take a moment to reflect on this definition.

- What is it saying to you?
- Which are the key words or phrases that stand out?
- Why are they important to you?

It's about striking a chord

In essence, influence is about handling other people's emotions effectively. It's about understanding how others are feeling and then using this knowledge in a way that enables them and you to move forward. Often this relates to achieving your desired outcome through the alignment of the desires of others.

Rookie Buster

Influence is about handling other people's emotions effectively.

However, it also relates to enabling others by simply giving them confidence, encouragement, direction or advice; or creating an environment that makes others feel good.

Through understanding others' feelings and perceptions, by exploring issues openly, and by adapting your behaviour and using language to build confidence, you can find ways to engage others, change behaviour and gain commitment to a cause.

Influencing others is sometimes said to be manipulative, but that's   135
only the case if what you are doing is not authentic and you have no
regard or respect for how the other person feels or what they want.

Why is influence important?

First and foremost, people are human. They have feelings just like you,
and while some may be more sensitive than others, all will be affected
in some way. Being attuned to how others are feeling means you have
the knowledge to tailor what you say and do to what is appropriate at
any given time.

Perhaps you need to avert a negative outcome, for example, by
allaying your team's fear of imminent change, reassuring a jealous colleague, or placating an angry, dissatisfied customer.

Or you need to enhance spirit and cohesion within your team,
perhaps by energizing individuals through discussing their role in the
project, promoting a good work/life balance within the team, or inspiring them through agreeing a goal and values.

When things are going really well, you can tap into the euphoria of
success: recognize and praise individual contributions, celebrate the
achievement, raise aspirations further, and set a new benchmark for
the team to achieve.

Identifying people's needs and addressing them effectively is
extremely powerful, and you will notice the effect on:

- Well-being.
- Energy levels.
- Creativity.
- Motivation.
- Performance.
- Team working.

Stop for a minute and think about a time when you
averted a bad outcome, enhanced a situation or acknowl-
edged an outstanding success.

What specifically did you do or say?

What impact did this have on the team or individual involved?

_____

_____

_____

Without influence, people often flounder – looking for direction or seeking leadership. Sometimes they struggle to make a decision, or need an injection of ideas, require information or basic support.

Some people willingly seek and invite help, but others won't have the courage or view it as a sign of weakness. These are the people who will often worry and suffer from anxiety and the effects of stress.

Therefore, influencing is important, but it is essential to recognize that others may be in a vulnerable position and you should respond to their needs with respect and empathy.

Exercise – How influential are you?

Have a look at the exercise below and consider how you may, knowingly or unknowingly, have influenced others in the past.

Below are a number of statements that can complete the sentence beginning "In the past, I have …". Place a tick in the shape alongside each statement that you feel describes what you have done.

… cheered someone up or distracted them from their problems by:
- Using appropriate humour.
- Telling jokes.
- Making fun of myself.

… frustrated or annoyed someone by:
- Teasing or mocking them.
- Being patronizing or putting them down.
- Performing a practical joke.
- Being sarcastic.

△ ... hurt and saddened someone by:
- Ostracizing them.
- Walking away.
- Being judgemental.
- Not listening.

☐ ... made someone feel valued by:
- Listening to them attentively.
- Spending time with them.
- Being affectionate, caring or sympathetic.

☐ ... calmed someone down by:
- Taking a slow, deliberate approach.
- Being passive.
- Avoiding criticism.
- Being non-confrontational.

△ ... intimidated others by:
- Slamming doors.
- Shouting.
- Arguing.
- Banging the desk.

△ ... made someone feel insignificant by:
- Ignoring them.
- Not using their name.
- Not greeting them when I've seen them.

☐ ... helped someone overcome their anxiety and feel happier by:
- Taking a rational approach to discussing an issue.
- Giving practical advice.
- Apportioning blame.
- Justifying actions.

△ ... upset and angered someone by:

- Criticizing a trivial thing.
- Challenging their opinion and belief.
- Comparing them to others.

☐ ... made someone feel proud and encouraged them to participate by:

- Paying them a genuine compliment.
- Giving them praise.
- Addressing them by name.
- Asking their opinion.

Add the number of ticks in each shape (square or triangle) and insert the totals below:

☐ statements indicate "I have influenced others positively."

△ statements indicate "I have influenced others negatively."

Compare the total in each shape and consider whether you are using your influence in a positive and genuine manner.

Personal reflection: Lessons I have learned about myself

Finally take a few minutes to draw out three key lessons you have learned about yourself, and record them here.

1. _____

2. _____

3. _____

What can affect your ability to influence?

Your ability to influence can be affected if you:
- Are not attuned to the feelings of others.
- Haven't built rapport.
- Find it difficult to express yourself emotionally.
- Are not flexible in your approach.

Being attuned to the feelings of others

Having the ability to sense what others are feeling or needing and to generally pick up the "vibe" of those around you is paramount. Without this you will be missing out on a considerable amount of data that can help you to change a subdued atmosphere within your team or alter the negative mood or state of an individual.

If you're not picking up on others' emotions and moods, take time to consciously learn how to do this, and you'll start to see how you can positively alter their job performance, creativity or the cohesion of others.

> **Tip:** Tune in to others. Regularly stop and look at the facial expressions and the body language of a colleague; listen to them talking and hear the tone of their voice and the words they are using. What do these tell you about how they are feeling?

Tip: Test out what others are feeling. Once you've identified what you think someone else is feeling, check by asking them – for example, "I get the feeling you are not really enthused at the moment – is that right?" See whether you are sensing correctly.

Using your rapport

As you have seen in Chapter 6, being empathetic enables you to develop rapport, and with this comes your ability to influence positively and effectively. Rapport allows you to engage in conversations at a deeper level, and to find out more about the real person – their feelings, values, beliefs, opinions, likes and dislikes.

Rookie Buster

Rapport allows you to engage in conversations at a deeper level, and to find out more about the real person.

Try sharing some personal information and see how others respond to you. Be genuine in your interest; if you are not interested, don't ask. Over time you will build up a level of confidence and trust that will positively enhance your working relationship.

Tip: Develop your questioning skills, and be brave. Ask those feelings-based questions, and listen. By getting under the skin of others, you may start to expose the real reason for their critical approach or negative mood.

Tip: Change someone's behaviour. If you notice that someone always seems to look cross, has hurried behaviour or a non-inviting expression, try smiling each time you see them and see how they respond to you.

Expressing yourself emotionally

Being emotionally expressive doesn't mean you need to be emotional. It means you need to express what you are feeling through your body language, your facial expressions, your voice and your words.

Rookie Buster

You need to express what you are feeling through your body language, your facial expressions, your voice and your words.

As you are aware, you can't help but leak your emotions through non-verbal means. However, what you can determine is whether leaking your negative emotion (anxiety or frustration, for instance) is useful at that moment or not. If it is, because others need to see it, feel it and respond themselves, then fine – show it.

Imagine you have a deadline to meet for your client, and you are anxious to get the data you need from your team on time. Let the team observe you scurrying around, let them see the focus and determination in your face, let them hear the shortness in your voice – there's no time for jokes or small talk right now. They will pick up the vibe that the pressure is on and will (assuming you have their trust, respect and support) respond accordingly.

Equally, when you have had good news and there's been a success for the team, use your positive emotion to your advantage and demonstrate your feelings of happiness, enthusiasm and energy. Smile openly

142 and widely, show your pride in the team, be relaxed, make time to chat over the success with individuals and verbalize what this result will mean for everyone in the future.

Being flexible in your approach

Everyone is different. How people respond differs depending on their specific drivers or motivational needs. Individuals have a particular style, work at their own pace, use their own set of words, and behave in certain ways.

Consequently, how you influence one person can be very different to how you influence another. You need to be flexible, understand who you are dealing with, and identify how best to approach them.

Rookie Buster

How you influence one person can be very different to how you influence another.

Then you need to shape your case. From a rational perspective, consider what's in it for them, as well as for you. Look for the win–win in any situation, based on what you know the other person wants, likes, dislikes, and so on.

Fundamentally, you need to appeal to the other person at an emotional level. So get the approach right, ensure the rationale is meaningful to them, and use appropriate language.

Getting real emotional commitment comes down to capturing the heart.

Tip: Increase your flexibility. Make a point of viewing things from other perspectives. Before making a decision, shape your understanding of the issue, and how it will be received by others, by putting yourself into their shoes and taking a look from their position.

Tip: Before any discussion of difficult issues, reflect on the individual's personality type, what motivates them, their style and preference, and think through what you will say and how you can engage them to achieve the best outcome for both parties.

How does your influence affect others?

Influencing others is easy if you have created the right environment and earned their respect.

Creating the right environment

Consider an environment in which:
- People can be open and honest.
- There is a willingness to share and collaborate.
- Ideas and opinions are sought.
- Feelings and concerns are shared.
- Everyone feels valued and respected.

In such an environment, your need to influence will be diminished as your style and approach will be in tune with your people.

144   Whenever you need to make a decision, you:
- Reflect on how the outcome might affect individuals or the team.
- Conduct a one-to-one conversation with each individual involved.
- Hold an open discussion.
- Listen to and explore the views of others.
- Consider the points raised.

Through this approach, and by seeing the perspective of others, understanding how they feel and how they react to the decision you make, you can become better informed.

Once you have made your decision you'll be able to explain your rationale, acknowledging the points raised by others, identifying those you considered, those you embraced and those you were obliged to disregard, remembering to explain why.

This is an environment in which people feel involved and become emotionally attached to the project and the team. In this environment you are much less likely to find resistance, as people know their voice has been heard and their inputs have been genuinely considered, and there is mutual understanding.

> **Tip:** If you involve others in shaping and informing your decision making, *always* provide them with your rationale for the final outcome, no matter how trivial it may seem to you.

Earning the respect of others

Influencing others comes down to respect. If you haven't earned respect, you won't have a chance. You may believe your position or title guarantees respect, but in the real world, it doesn't work like that.

Rookie Buster

If you haven't earned respect, you won't have a chance.

Here are four ways to ensure respect:

1. You need to show you have credibility by sharing your knowledge and experience openly and generously. Offer advice, be a sounding board or make time to mentor others.
2. Let others know that you don't know it all. Be honest, show your vulnerability and ask the "experts" for their help.
3. Ask *everyone* for their input, their feelings, their views and opinions. It's important to them to feel valued, respected and worthy, and important for you to receive the richness of their ideas and perspectives.
4. Build the confidence of others through the language you use. Words have power, and the way you use them will make all the difference to how others feel and how they respond to you.

Rookie Buster

Words have power, and the way you use them will make all the difference to how others feel and how they respond to you.

Exercise – Influencing through language

Listen carefully to the words you use every day and think about whether they are positive or negative, whether they build the confidence of others, whether they give others confidence in you, or whether they simply crush any belief or respect.

146   1. List the common words and phrases that you use – positive on the left and negative on the right.

Positive   *Negative*

_____   _____

_____   _____

_____   _____

2. Now look at the phrases below, and identify those that you could genuinely start to adopt.

"I recognize the effort you have put in to date."

"I know we will achieve what we set out to do."

"I am very positive about ..."

"I am committed to making this happen."

"I am confident we have turned the corner."

"I am really proud of what you have achieved."

"I truly believe that ..."

"We will absolutely smash those targets if we ..."

_____

_____

_____

3. Now identify other words and phrases that you would feel comfortable using.

_____

_____

_____

Beware! You have to mean what you say, and believe it yourself. **147**
Insincere words do more damage than saying nothing. Nobody is
fooled by insincerity. So be genuine, and only use words you believe
and are prepared to stand by.

Striking a chord: Bringing influence to life

Your starting point

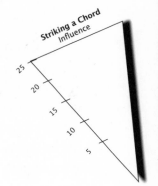

1. Transfer into this box your influence score from
   the EI self-perception questionnaire in Chapter 2.

2. Now that you know more about influence, re-evaluate this score
   and plot on the Striking a Chord blade above. This score is an
   indicator of your level of influence and is based on your self-
   perception.
3. Reflect on your entries in your emotions diary, and if you
   recognize there is scope for strengthening your influence, take
   some time here to jot down your ideas. You may like to think
   about this in terms of what you could *start*, *stop* and *continue*.
   - Start – for example, start identifying how my colleague is
     feeling, and then ask her to see how "tuned in" I really am.
   - Stop – for example, stop railroading others without giving
     them a chance to express their opinions or concerns.
   - Continue – for example, continue expressing my positive
     moods through what I do and say.
4. Use The Johari Window template in the Appendix and consider,
   in relation to your influence, how you behave and how you feel.

148   Jot down your behaviours (Box 1) and your feelings (Box 2).

5. Your influence will have an impact on others. To gain a true understanding of this, you need to ask others for their feedback. Identify four people who know you well in the workplace and use the five statements from the influence section of the EI questionnaire (page 37 in Chapter 2) as prompts for discussion with each of them. Their perceptions will provide valuable data – some may confirm your own perception, while some may differ.
6. Go back to The Johari Window template and in Box 1 capture the perceptions shared by you and others. Then complete Box 3 and record anything you had been previously unaware of. The real value of this exercise is discovering things you don't already know about yourself.
7. Based on your findings, revisit and, if necessary, revise your *start*, *stop* and *continue* actions.

    You can now bring your influence to life through the following personal development activities.

Personal development activities 149

1. Feelings-based conversation

Using feelings-based conversation may feel awkward and embarrassing, but if used with genuine care and with the intention of achieving a positive and productive outcome, it can be very powerful.

Sharing your feelings

If you wish to elicit a change in the behaviour of a colleague or team member, try an emotions-based approach. Explain in a calm and considered manner exactly how their behaviour makes you feel, and give an indication of how you would like them to behave.

For example, "I was very disappointed and quite upset that you didn't return my calls yesterday, after I'd left three messages. I always return my calls as soon as I get a message; it's a mark of respect."

Be careful which emotions you share. Think about the effect certain emotions may have on the other person. You need to create the right response to achieve a productive outcome.

For instance, in the example above, using "disappointed" and "upset" makes this personal to your emotions. It may seem as though you are putting yourself in a weaker position, but this is more likely to elicit empathy or sympathy from the other person, which then leads to an amicable and understanding conversation as well as a positive change in behaviour.

Saying "I was very frustrated and angry ..." might instead create a feeling of blame and tension. This could provoke conflict or inflame the situation, and then nothing would change.

> **Tip:** Enter such discussions with the outcome you wish to achieve already in mind, and remember that the outcome will be defined by your response to the situation. Outcome = event x response.

Encouraging others to share their feelings

Some people find it difficult to talk about feelings, and they may even consider it unprofessional or "soft" to do so in the workplace. However, if you can encourage conversation at a feelings level you may be able to open up the conversation, get to the root of an issue, and lead to mutually agreed actions.

For example, try saying, "I've been thinking about your situation and know it can't be easy for you that I have been brought in to lead this team. I am sure you're feeling rather frustrated and hurt by this – am I right?"

By suggesting what the other person may be feeling, you have given them the opportunity to either agree or deny. Either way, you can start to explore their true feelings and move on to what needs to happen to change their feelings, perception and behaviour.

Further exploration may follow, and could include:

- "So – what needs to happen now?"
- "What do you need to do?"
- "What would you like me to do?"
- "When shall we review?"

> **Tip:** Reflecting on how others are feeling is a good technique to encourage open feelings, and also to calm a potentially heated situation.

2. Gaining insight into other people's positions

How you perceive a situation determines how you feel about it, and therefore determines how you react or respond. It's natural to think that everyone is seeing and perceiving things in the same light. However, everyone is different, and their values, beliefs, personal experience and previous knowledge will all shape their view of an issue.

Of course, the very best way to find out what someone else is thinking and feeling is to openly discuss the situation. However, that may not always be possible, or you may want to gain an insight ahead of your discussion.

Rookie Buster

The very best way to find out what someone else is thinking and feeling is to openly discuss the situation.

To gain that insight into how others might be seeing a situation, try to put yourself into their shoes and look at it from their perspective. You'll be surprised at how much information you'll be able to gather and how your emotional responses will change.

Here's a technique for learning how to see things from someone else's perspective.

As you move through the three positions outlined below, physically move to a different position in the room and then jot down your responses to the questions below.

1. First position – your own personal point of view, seen through your eyes.
2. Second position – look through the eyes of the other person involved.
3. Third position – view the situation as if you were an observer watching both you and the other person involved.

Ask yourself:
- What have I learned?
- What new information do I now have?
- What feelings have I experienced?

You can use this technique to:
- Gather more information to understand where others are coming from before you start a discussion or try to influence another.

152

- Improve rapport by showing that you can see the other person's perspective.
- Change your perspective if you are feeling unsure.
- Give yourself some emotional distance.

3. Pacing and leading others

An effective way to build rapport and influence others is to synchronize yourself to their pace before you attempt to take the lead.

This means mirroring or matching their:

- Behaviour (body posture, gestures, stance).
- Breathing.
- Energy levels.
- Voice tone.
- Language (expressions, similar metaphors, echoing their views).

"Pacing" another person will help to make them feel that you are listening and you value what they say. It will begin to build trust and co-operation, so:

1. Observe the other person closely.
2. Watch out for their posture, expression, stance, speed of breathing and speech.
3. Decide which of these you want to pace.
4. Go at their pace.
5. Mirror their physical stance and movements in a subtle way (avoid mimicry).
6. Continue to pace until you see signs that they are at ease and you feel you have established rapport.
7. Now you can think about taking the lead.

You might want to take the lead in discussing a topic that you feel could be difficult. Once you have established rapport, you can introduce the potentially "sticky" topic, and you will be much more likely to find that you can explore it openly and without aggression, and find an effective and practical solution.

Coach's notes

Influencing is about engaging others at an emotional level. Being sensitive to an individual's feelings and needs helps you to adapt your communication in a way that makes that emotional connection.

- Arouse emotion in the other person and you'll be tapping into the heart. Persuading others with fact and opinion alone is not enough to engender real commitment.
- Inject humour (appropriately) and show your sense of fun to lighten the mood in difficult or tense situations.
- Be sincere and show your concern for others, and you'll foster warmth and build trust.
- Be realistic and optimistic. It's no good being overly enthusiastic and painting an unrealistic picture of the future when you know that doesn't reflect what is really going on.

Go for it! "Influencing others is not just a matter of pushing information at them, it's about creating an experience to engage the gut." *Adapted from John Seely Brown, chief scientist, Xerox Corporation*

Notes

Intuitiveness is a feeling or a sense of what is the best thing for you to do at the time. It's a perception of rightness or wrongness!

It's the feeling that you experience when buying a new house. The particular house that you are viewing has all the physical criteria that you are looking for (the right number of rooms, right size and location), but as soon as you walk through the door you know it "feels" wrong. The decision as to whether you buy it or not is based on what your "gut" tells you.

Listen to your feelings; they tell you what to do. As a child you have a strong sense of intuitiveness, but as you grow older you stop listening to it so much, and instead often listen only to the logical, analytical mind. The analytical mind is a valuable tool, but it needs to work in partnership with your intuitive mind as well.

CHAPTER 8

Trusting your inner voice

What is intuitiveness?

This chapter explores intuitiveness and why it's important. It provides you with the opportunity to try it out by using some very practical exercises. Developing and using your intuitiveness will give you:

- A self-checking system you can trust.
- A way of supporting yourself.

And by the end of this chapter you will not only understand the importance of tapping into your intuitiveness, but you will also value it as one of the most useful life skills that you can ever possess.

Higgs and Dulewicz define intuitiveness as: "The capability to arrive at clear decisions and drive their implementation when presented with incomplete or ambiguous information using both rational and 'emotional' or intuitive perceptions of key issues and implications."

Take a moment to reflect on this definition.

- What is it saying to you?
- Which are the key words or phrases that stand out?
- Why are they important to you?

158   It's about trusting your inner voice!

Intuitiveness is your ability to tap into the power of your intuition or your sixth sense (referred to here as your inner voice), and to make full use of it to enable you to make quicker and wiser choices or decisions. It is about using the combination of a solid knowledge base with the ability to "sense" what needs to be done, and then taking the required action.

An emotionally intelligent person learns to listen to their inner voice and trust the value that it brings.

Why is intuitiveness important?

Your "sense" or "gut feeling" may well be a remnant of an early warning system for danger, an apprehension or "gift of fear". The ability to think through your decisions and arrive at the "correct" answer is not enough: you also need to be able to acknowledge your gut feeling – that is, your instinctive, astute response.

Learning to work with your intuition isn't only necessary: it's vital to business and personal success. The ability to "sense" what is going on, and to collect and interpret the "soft" data (that is, feelings), is seen in the most emotionally intelligent business leaders. The most impressive of these leaders are those who have refined their intuitiveness – they can judge if relationships are working and pick up on non-verbal cues, and are able to use this information in formulating their response to challenging situations.

With the amount of information that floods the workplace today, making decisions based on all the rational facts could take a very long time indeed, so the ability to trust your judgement could give you a competitive edge in starting a new initiative or responding to a crisis. Around 80 per cent of senior managers use intuition when working in ambiguous situations, and often the more senior they are, the more they rely on their intuitiveness.

Rookie Buster

Learning to work with your intuition isn't only necessary: it's vital to business and personal success.

The importance of developing intuitiveness is that it enables you to deal with many situations. For example, someone with a high level of intuitiveness can:

- "Tune in" to the true nature of a person or situation.
- Make decisions in difficult situations.
- Build support for these decisions.
- Recognize that often it is more important to make a decision than to have all possible information available.
- Balance intuitive thinking with rational thinking.
- Reach a timely decision.

For example, Richard Branson, CEO of the Virgin Group, uses intuition to make decisions. If it feels right, he just does it. His book *Screw It, Let's Do It*, provides many of his personal, intuitive examples. It's a book worth reading.

What can affect your intuitiveness?

Your logical, analytical mind can!

When you focus on problems and churn them around and around in your head, it can feel like you're in a whirlpool. The swirling, bubbling water represents your analytical mind going over and over the problem. Often this leads to confusion and you may hear yourself saying, "I just can't think myself out of this one."

If this is the case, you need to engage your intuitive mind. This enables you to look beyond the turmoil, into the deeper, calmer water. Once you open your mind to explore these deeper parts of yourself and "listen" to what it might be telling you, you'll be surprised at how

160   many answers present themselves. Intuition supports and enhances logical decision making, enabling you to come up with quick solutions – and be able to trust in them.

Rookie Buster

> Intuition supports and enhances logical decision making, enabling you to come up with quick solutions.

You must stop the constant self-talk of your analytical brain and listen to your intuition. Trust that it is always there, letting you know what to do. Ask yourself, now, to what extent are you able to listen to your intuition, and how willing are you to act on it.

Another thing that can affect your intuitiveness is knowing that it exists, but choosing not to use it.

Ignore your intuitiveness at your peril! Not listening to or following your intuition may have caused you regret in the past. As you look back, you may recognize certain situations where you have done something or made a decision that has gone wrong. You can probably see that the "feelings" or "early warning" signals were there, but you didn't listen because they seemed irrational to you.

Exercise – When did you ignore your intuitiveness?

Take a moment to think of a time when this has happened to you.

Make a note of the circumstances; how you felt at the time; what convinced you to go with the decision that you did; and what was the outcome of taking this decision in both the short and long term?

_____

_____

_____

_____

Now go on to reflect on what you learned from that experience, and how you have applied it since.

_____

_____

_____

_____

Tip: pay attention to your feelings. Never ignore your body's signals: it could be telling you something really important. Those physiological tell-tale signs – the tingling feeling of happiness, the "pit of the stomach" feeling – whatever you experience, positive or negative, take notice!

The ability to trust your inner voice

As Gerd Gigerenzer, a cognitive scientist and author of *Gut Feelings: The Intelligence of the Unconscious*, says, "The question is not if, but when we can trust our guts." When faced with making a decision where you don't have all the necessary detail, Gigerenzer says that "it makes more sense to trust your intuition, with its evolutionary advantages, than your conscious brain".

162 "The lesson is to trust your intuition when thinking about things that are difficult to predict, and when you have little information," he says.

Rookie Buster

"It makes more sense to trust your intuition, with its evolutionary advantages, than your conscious brain."

Your intuition can also be relied upon in situations where you have experienced the same thing many times before. For example, if you are an experienced stockbroker you will make snap decisions as to where you should place an investment, or if you are an interviewer you "just know" when someone is right for the job. This is because you have experienced many similar occasions, and all the information is stored in the unconscious parts of your brain. You can then tap into this stored information later to make instant decisions without being aware of it.

Tip: Become an expert. You can enhance your intuitiveness by equipping yourself with more knowledge and experience – for example, if you want to make better financial decisions, find out as much information as you can on the subject. Your brain will store it all for later use.

Keeping things in balance

Intuition is not perfect. You can go with your "gut feeling" and find that it turns out not to be the right thing to do. As you have read earlier, it is unwise to use either logic or intuition to the exclusion of the other.

By using both logic and intuition in balance you can make "safer", wiser decisions.

163

Richard Broughton, president of the North Carolina-based Intuition Laboratories, advises that you use your intuition to home in on a narrow range of choices quickly, then turn to logic to help you decide between them. For example, in the "buying a house" scenario, go to your "gut feeling" first, asking yourself "Which of the houses did I warm to? Which of them had a good 'vibe'?" Then, once you have some examples to choose between, you can turn to logic to help you pick the best one. Ask yourself questions like "Which one is closest to the right size, location, etc.?"

Rookie Buster

By using both logic and intuition in balance you can make "safer", wiser decisions.

Trusting your inner voice: Bringing intuitiveness to life

Your starting point

1. Transfer into this box your intuitiveness score from the EI self-perception questionnaire in Chapter 2.

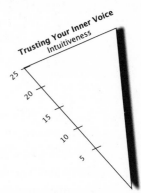

164   2. Now that you know more about intuitiveness, re-evaluate this
score and plot on the Trusting Your Inner Voice blade above. This
score is an indicator of your level of intuitiveness, and is based on
your self-perception.

3. Reflect on your entries in your emotions diary, and if you
recognize there is scope for strengthening your intuitiveness, take
some time here to jot down your ideas. You may like to think
about this in terms of what you could *start*, *stop* and *continue*.

- Start – for example, start being more confident in basing
decisions on my "gut feeling".
- Stop – for example, stop suppressing any intuitive feelings, and
instead listen to them.
- Continue – for example, continue being open minded about
using intuition.

4. Use The Johari Window template in the Appendix and consider,
in relation to intuitiveness, how you behave and how you feel. Jot
down your behaviours (Box 1) and your feelings (Box 2).

5. Your intuitiveness has an impact on others. To gain a true
understanding of this, you need to ask others for their feedback.
Identify four people who know you well in the workplace, and use
the five statements from the intuitiveness section of the EI
questionnaire (page 38 in Chapter 2) as prompts for discussion
with each of them. Their perceptions will provide valuable data –
some may confirm your own perception, while some may differ.

6. Go back to The Johari Window template, and in Box 1 capture the perceptions shared by you and others. Then complete Box 3 and record anything you had been previously unaware of. The real value of this exercise is discovering things you don't already know about yourself.

7. Based on your findings, revisit and, if necessary, revise your *start*, *stop* and *continue* actions.

You can now bring your intuitiveness to life through the following personal development activities.

Personal development activities

1. Assessing your intuitiveness

Here are three very simple, fun activities which will help you to see how intuitive you are.

Quick as a flash!
Intuitive people have the ability to name objects which they will have seen for only 1/25 of a second! How quick are you?

Ask a friend or colleague to show you a selection of different pictures and/or objects at speed, and you have to say what they are, as quickly as you can.

What's in a cloud?
Intuitive people make creative associations. This enables them to be open to new ideas and not to accept the first solution which comes to mind.

The easiest way to develop and practise this is to look at the clouds in the sky. Try to look beyond their physical shape and look at the picture within. Perhaps you did this as a child: "Hey, mum, look! That cloud looks just like a duck." Next time you are out, take a moment to glance up and look beyond the predictable.

166   **Freeze frame!**

Intuitive people have the ability to recall information that they weren't aware of learning. To practise this skill, you need to make a two or three minute recording of a crowd scene from a television programme.

Before watching the recording, you need to enlist the help of someone else. Ask them to watch the scene with you, and when the recording has stopped, switch the screen off and ask the other person to ask you questions about the scene.

Once you have responded to their questions, you can replay the scene and assess how accurate your observations were.

2. Listening to your intuition

This is an activity that you can try which helps you to really listen to yourself.

Step 1
The next time that you experience a feeling which seems to be acting as a warning, stop and take some deep breaths. Acknowledge how you are feeling and try to identify what that feeling is – is it confusion, anxiety, apprehension, excitement?

Step 2
Then find yourself a quiet place to do this exercise. Create a calming atmosphere; you may want to put some soft music on. Close your eyes and ask yourself, "What is the best thing that I can do about it right now?" The important thing to do now is to listen. Be quiet. Try to block out any of the internal chatter that you may have going on inside your head. Wait for your answer. Don't worry if nothing comes immediately: it will do when you are ready for it.

Step 3
Be sensitive to what you feel. Listen to the messages your body gives you. The answer may present itself in many ways, such as:
- You may feel it's just the right thing to do.

- It may come to you when you are thinking about something else.
- It may come as a small voice in your mind.
- It may come to you when you are talking to someone.
- It may just come to you in a flash.

Trust in the fact that you will know the answer when it comes.

Step 4
Act upon your intuition. Do it with confidence!

3. Freeing your intuitive spirit

What follows are some helpful questions which ask you to think about the decision you need to make in a way that will help to open your mind.

For this to work, you must trust your first impressions and believe in your answers! Go with the flow: you will be delighted with the results.

As you go through the exercise, write down your responses to each of the questions.

Here goes! Ask yourself:

- If this situation had a smell, what would it be?

_____

_____

- If this decision was a piece of fruit, how would it taste? How much juice would it have in it? Would I like to eat it?

_____

_____

168 • If this idea was making a sound, what would it be? Would it be tuneful or not?

_____

_____

• Before making the final decision, ask yourself, "How do I really feel about this?"

_____

_____

Another useful technique is, before taking any action, to take each option in turn and ask yourself the following questions:
• "If I take this option, how will I feel?"
• "If I don't take this option, how will I feel?"

Listen to the signals from your body, and choose the option that gives you the better feeling.

Coach's notes

Everyone possesses intuition, but only emotionally intelligent people tap into it and use it to improve both their decision-making and their relationships with others.

To continue developing and honing (or fine-tuning) your intuitive skills, you must:

- Trust in the fact that your intuition is always there, letting you know what to do.
- Be open minded and willing when trying to access your intuitive mind.
- Stop the constant internal chatter of your analytical brain and listen to your intuition.

Finally, remember that the key to making intuition work for you is to keep it in balance.

Go for it! Go on, be brave! It will take courage to trust your intuition, and the best ingredient to have is faith, not fear!

Notes

Being honest with yourself, keeping the promises you make to others, and upholding your own personal standards are all driven by your conscientiousness. When you feel uncomfortable about the way a discussion is going, or uneasy about a decision you have to take, it's a warning to you that your principles are being challenged.

Your conscientiousness can be considered as your guide. When you are attuned to what "feels right" and follow that instinct, you feel energized. Your emotions and physiology remain aligned with your intentions, and energy is not expended unnecessarily. Conversely, battling with your innermost beliefs is draining and causes stress. You experience this turmoil through feelings of unease or physiological signals such as a headache.

This chapter highlights the value of your underlying principles and the importance of exploring them with others when you are faced with a dilemma. Your principles may be different from others, but that doesn't make them any more or less important.

CHAPTER 9

Being true to yourself

What is conscientiousness?

This chapter helps you to strengthen your conscientiousness by:
- Doing what is right, and managing compromise when needed.
- Having the courage to say "No".
- Clarifying the expectations you have of others and that they have of you.
- Behaving consistently.
- Communicating with congruency.

Higgs and Dulewicz give this definition of conscientiousness: "The capability to display clear commitment to a course of action in the face of challenge and to match 'words and deeds' in encouraging others to support the chosen direction. The personal commitment to pursuing an ethical solution to a difficult business issue or problem."

Take a moment to reflect on this definition.
- What is it saying to you?
- Which are the key words or phrases that stand out?
- Why are they important to you?

174   It's about being true to yourself

In essence, conscientiousness is about listening to your conscience and having the integrity to stay true to yourself.

It's about being guided by your principles: personal standards, beliefs and values. These come from your inner self, and have been shaped and defined throughout your life, giving you a feeling of what's right and wrong, what's possible or impossible. These inner principles give you a sense of identity, provide a rationale and drive your actions.

Conscientiousness is about maintaining congruency between what you feel, what you say and what you do, and having the courage to follow things through in a way that you believe is appropriate.

Rookie Buster

Conscientiousness is about maintaining congruency between what you feel, what you say and what you do.

Why is conscientiousness important?

Conscientiousness helps you to determine the right thing to do in any given set of circumstances. An "internal processing" person naturally checks themselves against their own judgements and standards before making a decision or taking action.

They ask themselves:

- Is this the right thing to do in this situation?

- Does it reflect me in the way I would want it to?

- Will this send the right message?
- Do I feel comfortable about doing this?

When your beliefs, values, words and actions are all aligned, you feel calm and at ease. There is congruency between your emotional state, your physiology and your inner conscience.

Rookie Buster

When your beliefs, values, words and actions are all aligned, you feel calm and at ease.

When things are not aligned, you feel a sense of unease, agitation and discomfort. There is incongruency within. Then you need courage to explore these feelings, to face up to the reality of what is causing them, and to seek to address them. It may require a tough conversation and it may make you unpopular with others, but ultimately you will feel better and be able to continue to perform effectively.

Tip: If it is not natural for you to process information internally, seek feedback from others. Ask them how your proposed decision or action could be interpreted. Then decide if that is what you really want to project to others.

Conscientiousness is important in creating:
- A professional personal culture.
- A credible and trustworthy organizational culture.
- An environment where quality is of the highest order.
- A society where people care about others and the environment.

176   ## Exercise – Dealing with incongruent feelings

Your colleague is too busy to attend a meeting and has asked you to stand in for him. He's asked you to tell the client that he's off sick. You're not happy about this.

How would you feel?

_____

_____

_____

What would you do?

_____

_____

_____

What would you or your colleague need to do to make you feel happy with this situation?

_____

_____

_____

Illustrating high conscientiousness

People with high levels of conscientiousness:
- Set and adhere to high personal standards.
- Live by their values and do not compromise.

- Show great determination and "go the extra mile".
- Honour promises and deliver on the commitments they make.
- Are committed to achieving their desired outcome.
- Are disciplined in their approach.
- Take responsibility for their own actions and decisions.
- Continually improve – aim always to be and to do the best they can.
- Behave ethically – uphold professional rules and conform to norms.
- Are regarded as genuine and authentic.
- Are open and transparent in dealing with others.
- Treat others fairly.
- Show sincerity, integrity and emotional honesty.
- Are loyal and trustworthy.
- Show consistency in their approach, behaviour and words.

Exercise – How conscientious am I?

Think about your current projects or "to do" list and, taking each task in turn, consider how you feel in relation to the actions you have taken and need to take.

Identify those things that make you feel uncomfortable.

_____

_____

_____

Ask yourself:
Why do I feel uncomfortable?

_____

_____

_____

177

What do I need to do to make me feel at ease?

_____

_____

_____

What are the consequences if I don't address those things?

_____

_____

_____

Now reflect on your notes and ask yourself:
- What message does my action or inaction send to others?
- Is this how I want them to view me?
- On a scale of 1–10, how conscientious do I believe I am?
  Scale: 1...5–6.......................................10
  Poor   Average   Above average

Personal reflection: Lessons I have learned about myself

Finally take a few minutes to draw out three key lessons you have learned about yourself, and record them here.

1. _____

2. _____

3. _____

What can affect your   179
conscientiousness?

Your conscientiousness can be affected if:
- Your values or ethics are misaligned.
- You find it difficult to say "No".
- Expectations are not openly shared and discussed.

Aligning values and ethics

From time to time you will be faced with a dilemma that challenges your values and ethics. Perhaps it's a project with a new client in a business sector that you can't condone, such as gambling or smoking; perhaps it's an organization with a corporate responsibility policy that doesn't reflect your social or environmental views; or perhaps you need to work with a colleague whose values or standards are completely at odds with your own.

Whatever the situation, this dilemma will undermine your conscientiousness and cause you unnecessary angst and anxiety unless you can resolve it in some way.

Be brave and consider the situation carefully and its implications for:
- Your attitude and mood, and its impact on your self-belief and motivation.
- The way you behave, and the effect that has on others.
- Your health and well-being.
- Your commitment to the project.
- The quality of the work you deliver.
- Your promotion prospects.

Facing up to such dilemmas is not easy, but an emotionally intelligent person

180 knows that they need to find a solution that is acceptable to them and others involved. Being open and honest at an early stage may allow an early exit from the project; alternatively, find an acceptable compromise.

> **Tip:** Compromising your principles is not sustainable over prolonged periods. If you are in an environment where your conscientiousness is continually challenged; when you often have an uncomfortable or twisted feeling in your stomach, or regularly suffer from headaches, consider whether your personal values are really aligned to the organization's values. If they aren't, move on before your health suffers irrevocably and you become truly unhappy.

It is tough accepting a compromise when you hold strong beliefs, and it is important to develop a deep sense of self-awareness and strong emotional resilience. Develop strategies to change your state and overcome the inevitable feelings of discomfort, guilt and upset (see Chapter 3). Learn the breathing technique in Chapter 4 to manage your physiology and maintain coherence within.

Say "No" when you need to

Some people just can't say "No"! Sometimes this is personality driven – maybe you're a person who likes to please others or to help out, and who would not dream of saying "No" to a needy colleague or team member. But sometimes it's a case of learning how to say "No" or how to be more assertive when you really need to be.

Taking on more than you can reasonably deliver has negative consequences if you can't fulfil your commitments. If you deliver late or not at all, if you forget to follow through or simply run out of time, your credibility is undermined.

Excuses and further promises aren't enough. Even if others appreciate your good intentions, they perceive you as disorganized or unreliable. This reflects poor conscientiousness.

Tip: Be realistic and honest before committing yourself to take on a task. Think about the practicalities of what you need to do and the timeframe. Then stop and consider how you really feel – listen to your intuitive voice. What do you hear that voice saying? Also consider your physiology; if you feel your body temperature rising or feel sick, you are anxious; if you feel a lightness in your body, you are receptive.

Rookie Buster

Taking on more than you can reasonably deliver has negative consequences if you can't fulfil your commitments.

Share and discuss expectations

It is easy to assume that everyone has the same standards of personal conduct and that their expectations regarding the quality of work and client care are equal, but in reality this is not always the case.

Perhaps you feel uncomfortable and frustrated by the work ethic or attitude of others, or experience an uneasy feeling when you don't consider yourself to be the best person for a particular job. Maybe you question whether you are good enough or even worry that you always let others down.

Whenever anything jars with your conscientiousness, take note. Have the courage to face the issue. Openly discuss your expectations of others and find out their expectations of you. By clarifying what's

182 expected, you eliminate uncertainty and reduce the likelihood of disappointment. If you find your own expectations or self-imposed targets are too high, reduce the pressure you place on yourself.

Rookie Buster

Openly discuss your expectations of others and find out their expectations of you.

Tip: Manage expectations – ask others what they expect of you and set out your expectations of them. Openly discuss and clarify both sets of expectations.

Tip: Identify a set of operating standards or values for yourself and others – once expectations are shared, identify and agree standards, such as what's acceptable in terms of language, behaviour and quality of work.

How does your conscientiousness affect others?

Conscientiousness is about consistency and congruency in the language you use and the behaviour you model.

Being consistent, regardless of how you feel or the pressure you are under, gives others a sense of reassurance and builds their belief in you. They instinctively know how you are likely to react to a certain issue or handle their particular concern.

Showing consistency also increases respect and engenders trust, as people know exactly where they stand. They are also more likely to share their mistakes, rather than cover them up and hope you won't find out!

Rookie Buster

Being consistent, regardless of how you feel or the pressure you are under, gives others a sense of reassurance and builds their belief in you.

Congruency is important in delivering your message. Show your belief in a cause through your passion and drive. Engage others by letting them see, hear and feel this, so that they know you really care.

When your words, tone of voice and body language do not give the same message, others know. When it is apparent that you don't really believe in what you are saying, it is hard to get the support and commitment you need. Conscientiousness drives motivation, guides actions and enables you to uphold your values. By taking actions that support your words, you appear authentic and sincere. By modelling behaviour that you want others to adopt, and by introducing values you want others to operate by, you create a culture of conscientiousness that drives performance, engenders mutual respect and maintains business ethics.

Being comfortable with yourself enables transparency – an authentic openness to others about one's feelings, beliefs and actions – which in turn builds trust in others.

184 *Being true to yourself: Bringing conscientiousness to life*

Your starting point

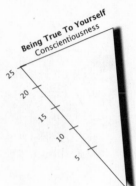

1. Transfer into this box your conscientiousness score from the EI self-perception questionnaire in Chapter 2.

2. Now that you know more about conscientiousness, re-evaluate this score and plot on the Being True to Yourself blade above. This score is an indicator of your level of conscientiousness, and is based on your self-perception.

3. Reflect on your entries in your emotions diary, and if you recognize there is scope for strengthening your conscientiousness, take some time here to jot down your ideas. You may like to think about this in terms of what you could *start*, *stop* and *continue*.

    *   Start – for example, having the courage to say "No" when I feel uncomfortable with what I am being asked to do.
    *   Stop – for example, stop accepting second best, and instead be clear about my expectations of others.
    *   Continue – for example, continue role modelling the behaviours I would like others to adopt.

4. Use The Johari Window template in the Appendix and consider,   185
   in relation to conscientiousness, how you behave and how you
   feel. Jot down your behaviours (Box 1) and your feelings (Box 2).

5. Your conscientiousness will have an impact on others. To gain a
   true understanding of this, you need to ask others for their
   feedback. Identify four people who know you well in the
   workplace and use the five statements from the conscientiousness
   section of the EI questionnaire (page 38 in Chapter 2) as prompts
   for discussion with each of them. Their perceptions will provide
   valuable data – some may confirm your own perception, while
   some may differ.
6. Go back to The Johari Window template and in Box 1 capture the
   perceptions shared by you and others. Then complete Box 3 and
   record anything you had been previously unaware of. The real
   value of this exercise is discovering things you don't already know
   about yourself.
7. Based on your findings, revisit and, if necessary, revise your *start*,
   stop and *continue* actions.

You can now bring your conscientiousness to life through the following personal development activities.

186 *Personal development activities*

1. Creating consistency

How you see yourself and how others see you varies enormously.

Your beliefs, values, standards and attitudes are determined by your inner self and are held within. Others cannot see these.

However, other people have a perception of who you are and what you believe in. They interpret what you say and do, and pick up on subtle nuances – your moods, attitude and the way you interact with others.

These messages create a picture of you. They set the tone for how others respond to you. Everyone sees you differently, depending on how you respond to them.

How others describe you may therefore differ from how you would describe yourself. Perhaps you believe you are loyal, reliable and fun. But would others say the same?

Take some time to complete this exercise. It requires your interaction with others who know you well. You may be in for some surprises. And it may explain why you don't always have the response you expect, the support you require or the fun you would like.

Step 1
Think of three words that describe you well. (These are your "descriptors".)

Step 2
Now ask at least five other people, independently and without being prompted, to think of three words of their own to describe you. These other people may be:

- A partner.
- Friends.
- Family members.
- Colleagues or peers.
- Others who report directly to you at work.
- Clients.

Ask each person to write down the three words. Ensure you can 187
identify who says what – you'll need to know this later.

Step 3
Review all the words used to describe you, and identify those words
that are the same or similar, and which appear three or more times.

Take this as your common set of descriptors, and compare it with
your own descriptors.

Reflect on the following questions:
- Do others see me as I see myself?
- What surprises me?
  - What do others see that I don't value in myself?
  - What don't others see in me that I value in myself?
- What descriptors are unique to certain relationships?
  - What do I do that gives that person that impression?
  - What do I need to do differently in that relationship?
  - What could I do differently in other relationships?

Reflect on what you have learned about yourself, and consider any
inconsistencies in your behaviour. Identify what you can do to change
perceptions by strengthening your conscientiousness.

Remember, how others react to you is determined by the impression that you give them.

2. Defining your values

Your personal values are at the heart of your conscientiousness. They
influence what you do and why you do it. It is the integrity to stay true
to your values when faced with dilemmas that differentiates the emotionally intelligent person.

188   1. Reflect on your inner values and identify three that you believe to
          be your core values.

_____

_____

_____

If you find it difficult to identify your values, try asking
yourself the question "What really matters to me and makes me
feel good?"

For example, maybe you enjoy working on new projects that
stretch you and that are outside your comfort zone, both
intellectually and emotionally – if so, you might identify
"continual improvement" as one of your core values.

Alternatively, ask yourself, "What do I find annoying about
how others behave, or the things they say?"

Perhaps you get frustrated when other people arrive late for
meetings, are not prepared and don't seem to care about how they
present themselves. If so, you might identify "professionalism" as
one of your core values.

2. Now define what you actually mean by this value. What would
    you be doing or seeing if you were displaying this value?

    For example:

    - Enjoyment – having fun; working in a sociable environment.
    - Co-operation – being part of a team; working closely with
      others.
    - Uniqueness – being different; standing out from the crowd.

Coach's notes

Have the courage to be true to yourself and to be a role model for others.

Be true to yourself

- Show passion for your beliefs, and stand by your principles.
- Recognize any feelings of unease or inner conflict, and address them.
- Ask others what they expect from you – then you know if you are meeting their expectations.
- Recognize what you can and cannot do. Be open with others about them.
- Always deliver on your promises; create the time you need to ensure that you can deliver.
- Demonstrate integrity and ensure that you do what you say you will do. Ask others for their perception.
- Be accountable. Set milestones and measures. Openly share what you are doing with others and review progress.

Be a role model

- Be consistent in your behaviour, and show congruency when delivering a message. Your words, tone of voice and body language must be aligned.
- Check what others have heard, when communicating; don't assume everyone has got the right message.
- Be open and honest in terms of your expectations of others.
- Demonstrate your passion always to be and to do your best.
- Be fair; treat everyone the same.
- Appreciate cultural differences, and learn to accept them and to work with others.
- Recognize that the values and beliefs of others will differ from your own; therefore discuss and agree minimum operating standards.
- Demonstrate that you are prepared to do yourself what you ask of others.

Go for it! Live by your values and principles, and act with conviction and authenticity.

Notes

At the beginning of this book you were asked to think about someone who positively affects you; someone who "stands out from the crowd"; someone whose personal qualities and attributes truly inspire you.

Essentially what this person does is create a culture through the way they behave; an emotionally intelligent culture that engages others and that has a lasting impact.

So – how would *you* like to have this effect on others?

CHAPTER 10

Creating your personal culture

"I create the culture that I behave"

Being emotionally intelligent not only enables you to have a happier, healthier and more successful life, but it also allows you to help others achieve the same. As the great German poet Goethe once said, "Treat people as if they were what they ought to be, and you help them to become what they are capable of being."

Now you have read this book, you are more aware of how your emotional intelligence can shape the way you think, feel and act. You know how you can affect others and how you can create and sustain an inspiring environment where others want to be.

However, this knowledge and understanding is not enough. If you really want to make a difference, you need to embrace emotional intelligence and live it!

Adopt the phrase "I create the culture that I behave" as your first principle of emotional intelligence, and recognize that you can change an outcome by adapting your responses.

194

Rookie Buster

If you really want to make a difference, you need to embrace emotional intelligence and live it!

Inspire others

When you adopt the principles and strategies of this book, you become a role model for emotional intelligence.

Others see you behave in a manner that is consistent and appropriate. They feel supported, included and valued. They regard you as someone who has time to listen to their thoughts; who understands their feelings; and who works with them to find a solution to a problem.

They allow themselves to be influenced by you: you involve them in the decision-making process, and they take ownership of achieving the goal.

As a result, you create a culture of positive energy where you and others are motivated to achieve fantastic results. EI development is a journey of surprises and moments of epiphany.

Your next steps

You've now reached the final chapter of *Emotional Intelligence for Rookies*, and you might be excused for thinking that you are nearing the end of your EI journey.

Not so! In fact, this is only the *first stage* of your journey. It's now time for you to consider your next steps. How can you continue to develop your emotional intelligence? How do you now bring it to life?

Emotional Intelligence for Rookies has brought you this far, but now it's time for you to embrace EI, adopt it, and get on your way. You have to accept it as an ongoing process of development. It isn't something that you just pick up from time to time and put down again: it has to become your way of life, the way you conduct yourself and interact with others on a minute-by-minute, day-by-day basis for ever!

Remember – your success in applying the lessons which you have learned relies totally on your willingness and commitment to do so.

To help you on your way

The following models provide you with a framework for adopting and integrating EI into your everyday life.
- The adoption strategy.
- The integration model.

1. Adoption strategy

When adopting your new or improved way of behaving, manage yourself through this five-stage process.

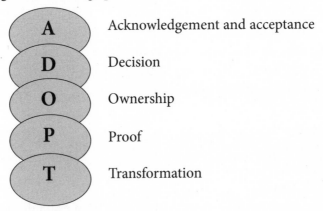

A   Acknowledgement and acceptance

D   Decision

O   Ownership

P   Proof

T   Transformation

Acknowledgement and acceptance
The first stage is to acknowledge and accept that in order to be emotionally intelligent you need to make changes in the way you behave. With this acceptance comes the motivation and commitment to put your learning into practice.

Using your enhanced self-awareness, feedback from others and information from the personal development activities throughout the book, make a note here of these things that you acknowledge and accept for change.

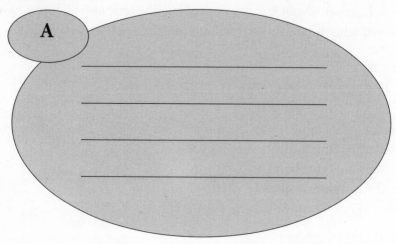

Decision

The second stage is to make a decision to commit to action.

As Ernest Hemingway once wrote, "Never confuse motion with action." Simply saying "I've decided to change the way I do things" is not enough. It implies good intentions, but it doesn't provide you with specific actions which you need to make the changes you want.

This is the point where you set yourself SMART goals.

A SMART goal is one which is:

Specific.

Measurable.

Achievable.

Relevant.

Time-related.

Now, using the following SMART goal as an example, write one of your own in the space provided.

For example: "To have a positive impact on the atmosphere in the office, each day when I first arrive, I acknowledge everyone personally, with a smile and a sincere greeting."

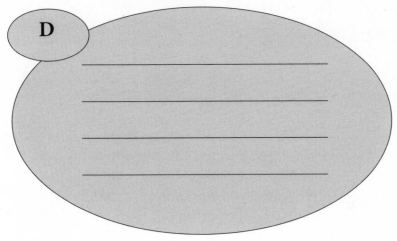

Ownership

Once you have set your SMART goals, you have to own their outcome. If you don't make it happen, it won't!

Some of your goals will take longer to achieve than others, and you may falter: don't worry if you do, and don't give up. Chapter 5 (Staying on Track) will help you with this. It is a time when you need to employ your strategies for self-motivation. Keeping sight of your long-term outcome whilst focusing on the short-term goals is going to be key at this stage. Ask others for feedback; this gives you support and encouragement. Don't forget to recognize your achievements, acknowledge them and reward yourself appropriately.

Rookie Buster

Keeping sight of your long-term outcome whilst focusing on the short-term goals is going to be key.

Write down a personal commitment to yourself.

198   For example: "Whenever I feel disheartened, think of three positive things that have happened to me that day."

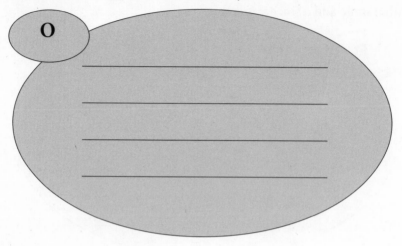

Proof

This stage is about gathering positive evidence of your emotional intelligence. Having this bank of information provides you with a resource that you can draw on should your self-belief be diminished for any reason.

When you recognize that your behaviour is less than emotionally intelligent, stop and reflect on the proof of where you have behaved differently. Use your positive internal chatter to change your attitude, thoughts, feelings and behaviour.

Gather your proof and note it down.

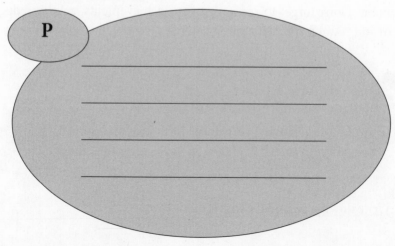

Transformation

The final stage is when you have fully adopted emotional intelligence as an integral part of yourself. This creates your personal culture.

You no longer have to think about what you are saying or doing, because it is all happening naturally. At this stage you are no longer a rookie – instead you will be a master!

A technique that you can use here is to create your future history.

Imagine yourself in the future as a Master of EI. Take a good look at yourself. What thoughts would be going through your mind? What would you be doing? What would you hear yourself saying? Note down your responses, then make a promise with yourself to come back and review your progress.

A useful way of reminding yourself of your commitment is to write these responses in a letter to yourself. Seal them in a stamped envelope addressed to you, give it to a trusted friend and ask them to post it to you in 3–6 months' time. If you have been applying your emotional intelligence, you will be amazed at what you'll see when you receive the letter.

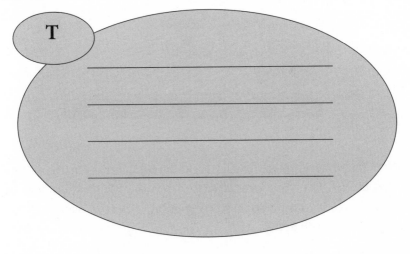

200   2. The EI Integration Model

The Integration Model merges the two key precepts of EI:

1. Everyone is emotionally intelligent to some degree
Everyone has a natural starting point for their EI development journey. It is unique to each person, depending on their age and life experience.

2. Emotional intelligence can be developed
Everyone has the capacity and potential to improve their emotional intelligence through knowledge, understanding and practice.

This model illustrates how EI improves over time.

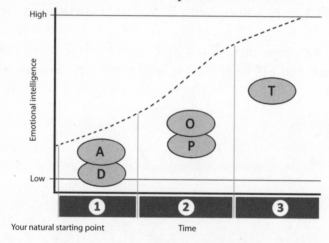

Note that different people will have different natural starting points on this model. Use your overall score from the EI questionnaire in Chapter 2 to plot your personal starting point. Wherever you start, the same principles still apply.

1. Start out
In this first phase of your development you will read and acquire knowledge over a short period of time. This gives you an insight into emotional intelligence, what it means, why it's important, and how to practise and continuously develop it.

During this phase you reflect on what you read and learn about yourself.

Through an increased understanding you automatically start to practise some of the behaviours, and become more self-aware and conscious of what you say and do.

2. Put EI into practice

In this second phase, you continue to work hard to adopt EI behaviours. You reflect on your ability, your successes and your setbacks. You re-align your personal EI goals by continuously using personal reflection and feedback from others.

As you continue to move through this phase you build belief and confidence and improve your self-esteem.

3. Be emotionally intelligent

Now that *you* are emotionally intelligent, you notice the difference in your personal performance and you successfully work with and through others. You feel at ease; it comes naturally and is an intrinsic part of you.

Your conscientiousness sets a standard that others aspire to, and you can now focus on enabling *their* EI development.

Go for it! There's only one thing left to say now – go for it, and good luck!

Appendix

The seven elements of emotional intelligence

1. Self-awareness
The awareness of one's own feelings, and the capability to recognize and manage these feelings in a way which one feels that one can control. This factor includes a degree of self-belief in one's capability to manage one's emotions and to control their impact in a work environment.

2. Emotional resilience
The capability to perform consistently in a range of situations under pressure and to adapt behaviour appropriately. The capability to balance the needs of the situation and task with the needs and concerns of the individuals involved. The capability to retain focus on a course of action or need for results in the face of personal challenge or criticism.

3. Motivation

The drive and energy to achieve clear results and make an impact, and also to balance short- and long-term goals with a capability to pursue demanding goals in the face of rejection or questioning.

4. Interpersonal sensitivity

The ability to be aware of, and take account of, the needs and perceptions of others when arriving at decisions and proposing solutions to problems and challenges. The capability to build from this awareness and achieve the commitment of others to decisions and action ideas. The willingness to keep open one's thoughts on possible solutions to problems and to actively listen to, and reflect on, the reactions and inputs from others.

5. Influence

The capability to persuade others to change a viewpoint, based on the understanding of their position and the recognition of the need to listen to this perspective and provide a rationale for change.

6. Intuitiveness

The capability to arrive at clear decisions and drive their implementation when presented with incomplete or ambiguous information, using both rational and "emotional" or intuitive perceptions of key issues and implications.

7. Conscientiousness

The capability to display clear commitment to a course of action in the face of challenge, and to match "words and deeds" in encouraging others to support the chosen direction. The personal commitment to pursuing an ethical solution to a difficult business issue or problem.

Useful tools

The Johari Window

Developed in the 1950s by American psychologists Joseph Luft and Harry Ingram, The Johari Window is a useful tool for understanding how you perceive yourself and how others perceive you.

In the context of emotional intelligence, The Johari Window allows you to see the impact that your emotions have on yourself and others. This helps clarify your thoughts, and enables you to make informed decisions about how you want and need to behave.

There are four different dimensions to this model which are set out as panes, (hence the window reference), and by exploring each of them you can learn more about yourself and your relationships with others.

Familiarize yourself with the four different panes.

1. Known to self and others
This is the open view of you; it's information that you recognize in yourself and that others see in you. It's what you say and what you do.

For example, maybe you know and everyone else knows that you lose your temper easily.

2. Known only to self but not to others
This is your private self, where you hide emotions and feelings that you are experiencing, and things that you are unwilling to share with

206   others. Perhaps you do this because you don't want to appear vulnerable or "out of control".

For example, maybe you hate losing your temper because it frustrates you; you feel others are able to control their tempers and it leaves you feeling disappointed in yourself.

3. Known to others but not to self

This area is all about the things you do, the way you look, your gestures, your posture and so on, which others are aware of but you are not! It is your blind spot. You may be blissfully unaware of what is happening. This is the essential area to explore for feedback, in order to find out the impact you are having, both positive and negative.

For example, maybe others think you look agitated, stressed or lost in thought, even though you don't realize it.

4. Unknown to self and others

This is your unknown self about whom nobody knows – least of all you!

For example, your unconsciousness, or feelings that you have not registered as, so far, there has been no trigger for them.

To maximize the use of this tool:

- Open up and share how you feel with someone else, to help them to understand you better.
- Ask for feedback from others. It's a fantastic way of opening your eyes to your blind spot. It expands your self-awareness and increases your open area (Box 1).

As you gain more insight into yourself, you start to develop your awareness of your unconscious emotions and, in time, you will be able to complete Box 4.

1. Known to self and others *How I behave*	3. Known to others but not to self *What others see me do or hear me say*
2. Known only to self but not to others *How I feel*	4. Unknown to self and others

The Johari Window template

208 The CardioSense Trainer

The CardioSense Trainer™ (or CST) is an electronic device that includes a unique breath pacer: this allows you to master the rate and the rhythm of your breathing (see Chapter 4). Breathing rhythmically at 6–8 breaths per minute at rest seems to be the optimum rate to bring coherence to your physiology and start to develop your emotional resilience.

The CST monitors the changes in your heart rate with a device called a "pulse wave sensor" and provides live feedback. The sensor clips to your ear lobe and detects your heart beat at the ear. The software then calculates the changes in your heart rate and displays this as a heart rate "tachogram" or picture on your computer screen.

By using the CST, you can:

- Learn how to control your breathing.
- Control your physiology and improve your heart rate variability.
- Learn to rapidly control your emotional state.
- Identify what events disrupt your physiology.
- Learn to create an optimum performance state.
- Enhance your own brain function.
- Track your own progress over time.

To find out more or to purchase your CardioSense Trainer, log on to http://www.cardiac-coherence.com

Useful books

Richard Branson; *Screw It, Let's Do It*; Virgin Books, London, 2006

Jane Cranwell-Ward, Andrea Bacon & Rosie Mackie; *Inspiring Leadership: Staying Afloat in Turbulent Times*; Thomson, London, 2002

Malcolm Gladwell; *Blink – The Power of Thinking Without Thinking*; Penguin Books, London, 2006

Daniel Goleman, Richard Boyatzis & Annie McKee; *The New Leaders: Transforming the Art of Leadership into the Science of Results*; Little, Brown, London, 2002

Genie Z. Laborde, *Influencing with Integrity: Management Skills for Communication and Negotiation*; Crown House Publishing, Carmathen, 2003

Andy Milligan & Shaun Smith; *See Feel Think Do: The Power of Instinct in Business*; Marshall Cavendish Business, London, 2008

Joseph O'Connor; *NLP Workbook: A Practical Guide to Achieving the Results You Want*; Thorsons, London, 2001

Geetu Orme; *Emotionally Intelligent Living*; Crown Publishing, Carmathen, 2001

Patsy Rodenburg; *Presence: How to Use Positive Energy for Success in Every Situation*; Penguin Books, London, 2007

Acknowledgements & sources

Acknowledgements

Material and "Describing your feelings" exercise in Chapter 2 reproduced by kind permission of Dr Alan Watkins, BSc MBBS PhD, Cardiac Coherence Ltd.

"Assessing your willingness to learn" exercise in Chapter 3 reproduced by kind permission of Katrina Rose, Inspire Development Ltd.

Self-belief cycle in Chapter 3 reproduced by kind permission of Katrina Rose, Inspire Development Ltd.

CST tachograms and breathing technique in Chapter 4 reproduced by kind permission of Dr Alan Watkins, BSc MBBS PhD, Cardiac Coherence Ltd.

Material referenced in "What drives me?" exercise in Chapter 5 drawn from Human Motivation by David C. McClelland, by kind permission of Cambridge University Press.

Material in the "Listening actively" section in Chapter 6 adapted by kind permission of Lynne Copp, The Work/Life Company Ltd.

"Gaining insight into other people's positions" activity and "Pacing and leading others" technique in Chapter 7 adapted and reproduced by kind permission of Ian McDermott, founder of International Teaching Seminars.

"The seven elements of emotional intelligence" shown in the Appendix and used as an overall framework for this book reproduced by kind permission of Professors Malcolm Higgs and Victor Dulewicz.

The Johari Window material in the Appendix reproduced by permission of The McGraw-Hill Companies.

Sources – books

Fiona Beddoes-Jones; *Thinking Styles – Relationship Strategies that Work!*; BJA Associates; Lincoln, 1999

James Borg; *Persuasion – The Art of Influencing People*; Pearson Education; Harlow, 2004

Jane Cranwell-Ward, Andrea Bacon & Rosie Mackie; *Inspiring Leadership: Staying Afloat in Turbulent Times;* Thomson; London, 2002

Daniel Goleman; *Working with Emotional Intelligence*; Bloomsbury Publishing; London, 1998

Daniel Goleman, Richard Boyatzis & Annie McKee; *The New Leaders: Transforming the Art of Leadership into the Science of Results*; Little, Brown: London 2002

Malcolm Higgs & Victor Dulewicz; *Making Sense of Emotional Intelligence*; ASE: London, 2002

Genie Z. Laborde; *Influencing with Integrity; Management Skills for Communication and Negotiation*; Crown House Publishing; Carmarthen, 2003

Ian McDermott & Wendy Jago; *The NLP Coach*; Judy Piatkus (Publishers); London, 2001

David Maister, Charles Green & Robert Galford; *The Trusted Advisor*; Simon & Schuster UK; London, 2002

Michael Neill; *Feel Happy Now!*; Hay House; New York, 2007

Richard Nelson-Jones; *Introduction to Counselling Skills*; Sage Publications; London, 2006

Joseph O'Connor & John Seymour; *Training with NLP*; Thorsons; London, 1994

Mike Pegg; *The Positive Workbook*; Enhance; Leamington Spa, 1995

Candace B. Pert; *Molecules of Emotion – Why you feel the way you feel*; Pocket Books; London, 1999

Patsy Rodenburg; *Presence: How to Use Positive Energy for Success in Every Situation*; Penguin Books; London, 2007

Tim Sparrow & Amanda Knight; *Applied EI*; John Wiley & Sons; Chichester, 2006

Sources – articles

Stanley Bass; "Energy - how acquired and lost in the body"; http://www.drbass.com/energy.html

Stanley Bass; "The relation between energy and feeling and thought" – extract from *Overcoming Compulsive Habits*; http://www.drbass.com/feeling.html

BBC Science & Nature Section, Human Body & Mind, Sleep; http://www.bbc.co.uk/science/humanbody/sleep

Bruce Charlton; review of *The Feeling of What Happens: Body, Emotion and the Making of Consciousness* by Antonio Damasio; 2000; www.hedweb.com/bgcharlton/damasioreview.html

Daniel Goleman; "How emotions matter for health"; http://toysgames4kids.wordpress.com/2007/12/14

212

Godfrey Golzen; "Executives with EQ (not IQ)"; *HR Magazine*; April 1999

Greg Landry; "Your eight hormones and weight loss"; Life Tools for Women, Section: Heath & Wellbeing; http://www.lifetoolsforwomen.com/w/8-hormones.htm

Loughborough University, Department of Human Sciences, Clinical Sleep Research Unit, Popular Articles; http://www.lboro.ac.uk/departments/hu/groups/sleep/

Karen Niven, Institute of Work Psychology & ESRC Centre for Organisation and Innovation, University of Sheffield; "What is emotional influence?"; http://www.sheffield.ac.uk/content/1/c6/07/11/56/emotional_influence.pdf

Stephanie Noble; "Emotions as honored guests"; extract from *Tapping the Wisdom Within, A Guide to Joyous Living*; Inside Out Books; 1994

Kacper Postawski; "How to create energy from nothing"; February 2007; http://mental-works.blogspot.com/2007/02/how-to-create-energy-from-nothing-lot.html

Kacper Postawski; "Powerful sleep – secrets of the inner sleep clock"; 2004; http://www.bouncebackfast.com/sleep/2sleepchapters.pdf

David Reilly & Tansy Harrison; "Creative consulting: psychoneuroimmunology, the mindbody"; *Student BMJ: Education*, Volume 10; April 2002

The Swiss National Centre of Competence in Research for the Affective Sciences; "What are affects and emotions? How do they work?"; www.affective-sciences.org/emotion-overview

Paige Waehner; "How to generate energy"; December 2004; http://exercise.about.com/cs/cardioworkouts/ht/generateenergy.htm

Extracts from interviews with EQ experts, including Jack Mayer, Eric Jensen, Candace Pert, Anabel Jensen, Maurice Elias, John Steinberg and J.-P. Dupreez; "What are emotions?"; *EQ Today*; www.eqtoday.com/archive/emotions.html

Index